BEYOND CULTURAL DIVERSITY

THE CASE FOR CREATIVITY

BEYOND CULTURAL DIVERSITY

THE CASE FOR CREATIVITY

A THIRD TEXT REPORT

COMPILED AND EDITED BY
RICHARD APPIGNANESI

ThirdText
Publications

First published in 2010 by
Third Text Publications
PO Box 3509, London NW6 3PQ

This book has been commissioned
By the diversity team at the
Head Office of Arts Council England
14 Great Peter Street
London SW1P 3NQ

ISBN 978-0-947753-11-5

British Library Cataloguing and Publications Data
A catalogue record for this book is available from the British Library

Supported by

ARTS COUNCIL
ENGLAND

Contents

Acknowledgements

We are grateful to Tony Panayiotou and Hassan Mahamdallie for their support in commissioning this *Third Text* Report.

The views expressed in the Report are the authors' responsibility and do not necessarily reflect those of the Arts Council England or *Third Text* magazine.

Our thanks to Yvie Andrews, Richard Dyer and Zoë Petersen for their editorial assistance in the production of this book. We are also grateful to the artists and artists' estates for their kind permission to reproduce the artworks illustrated in the *Third Text* Report.

Preface
The Creative Case for Diversity in the Arts

Diversity and arts have always existed. The need to express visually, in word, dance and movement is a human need and fulfils a fundamental drive. If it really is the case that everyone has a cultural entitlement and an inalienable right to participate and create in the arts, whether they choose to exercise that right as either creators or consumers (or not at all), leads inevitably to a simple supposition, that art is for everyone. Could it be that art then is an a priori human right crucial to our existence, even survival?

In this publication, *Third Text*, Arts Council England and our contributors set out to examine and analyse a number of key issues relating to diversity, equality and the arts. This is important and timely for a number of reasons, one of the most important being the development of the Arts Council's ten year vision for the arts *Achieving Great Art for Everyone*. There has been extensive public consultation on this and we have looked closely at what the public have said. Responses on matters of diversity and equality have provided a welcome endorsement of the work we have done so far. However, this publication aims to go further than just accepting that diversity and equality are good for the arts. There is a need for a fuller and deeper articulation than a simple, rather righteous statement gives.

Arts Council England approached *Third Text* in 2009 with an offer of a partnership to work together to take the debate about diversity and the arts to a new and different level. *Third Text* is a unique organisation, not without its criticism of the Arts Council, or indeed of its diversity interventions. It has, however, many years of high level advocacy for the arts and for championing a reinterpretation of the arts and its written history. *Third Text* has argued with passion and conviction that the Western analytical paradigm of the arts is distorted in its history and imposing in its values and aesthetics. This has led to the neglect of crucial Modernist work produced by black artists in Britain during the first decades of the postwar era. Here, in *Third Text*'s view, was a genuinely 'culturally diverse' model of art, and it remains largely ignored. It is their view that in this negligent collective failure by the arts establishment, firstly to recognise and value the diversity of cultural influences on British art, and secondly by erecting artificial barriers (social and economic as well as cultural/artistic) to keep this work at the periphery, has hurt all art and all those who enjoy the arts. As George Bernard Shaw put it (in his preface to *Androcles and the Lion*):

> We are members one of another; so that you cannot injure or help your neighbour without injuring or helping yourself.

Inversely, anything that opens up, democratises and addresses the historical influences and cultures within our art is going to be of benefit to all the arts community, the wider public and to the creative process.

That the Arts Council has a leadership role in such a movement is beyond debate. Amongst other things, Arts Council England has legal public duties under equalities legislation. Over recent years the key influences for our work on diversity and equality have been driven by a number of 'cases': the legal case (meeting public duties), the moral case (it is the right thing to do), the ethical case (it is the fair thing to do) and the business case (good for the box office). This publication does not criticise these approaches but there is a clearer, simpler and more potent position to articulate for greater diversity and equality in the arts – they are crucial to the arts by sustaining, refreshing, replenishing and releasing the true potential of England's artistic talent regardless of people's background. The benefits to the arts and cultural industries of unlocking this creativity, eradicating exclusion and having an arts sector which is truly welcoming and focussed on people is potentially magnificent.

This publication has been produced to provoke and stimulate a wider debate within the arts community and beyond and to provide a platform that invites everyone – regardless of gender, race, economic circumstance, sexuality and disability – who cares about the future of the arts, whether as arts practitioners and professionals, funders and the public, to make their contribution. The Arts Council welcomes your views. As an organisation we will be looking to build on this initial phase of the Creative Case to make good and informed decisions in all aspects of our policy-making and practices.

We hope too that organisations and artists that we fund engage with this work, organise workshops and discussion groups and help to create a lively debate that will help us respond to the challenges and opportunities ahead.

Tony Panayiotou
Director of Diversity
Arts Council England

Introducing the Creative Case

Ronald Moody, (b 1900, Kingston Jamaica – d 1984, London, England), *John the Baptist*, 1936, elm, 155 x 74 x 40 cm, collection: Tate

INTRODUCTION
'Whose Culture?'
Exposing the Myth of Cultural Diversity

Richard Appignanesi

Culture is by nature diverse. Diversity, or some would propose hybridity, is the lifeblood of culture. I am speaking of diversity as a condition inherently *within* cultures and not simply of the obvious differences *between* them. Apparently this fact needs to be recalled. And for good reason, since the officially sanctioned policy of cultural diversity at present confuses the issue of whose culture is being differentiated. The notion of cultural diversity in its current administrative form does not rightly acknowledge that culture within itself is already an assemblage of differences, diverse tendencies and unresolved tensions, but is instead focused primarily on the strains of separation between cultures. I should emphasise that in this view of cultural diversity the strains of disquieting difference come from the 'ethnic minority' cultures, those unsettled and problematic guests in the midst of the host mainstream culture. Mainstream, of course, meaning Western, European and predominantly white; and mainstream also implicitly presuming itself wholly unified and homogeneous. Diversity from this viewpoint is disruptive, an upset of status quo normality, which must somehow be governed so that the mainstream culture can function undisturbed by any threat of 'difference' from the inside.

Let us be clear. Cultural diversity is a meaningless tautological expression. It tells us nothing but that cultures differ. Something other is hidden behind this mere description. The empty formulation of cultural diversity disguises a prescriptive conduct. We can understand cultural diversity as a sort of foreign policy intended for domestic application. Perhaps this way of looking at it will bring strikingly home to us the question: why is there an officially differentiated category of diverse cultures for some citizens who are undeniably in the fabric of British society? Some of us in Britain are being cast as outsiders who require a domestically engineered foreign policy. The question profoundly concerns the integrity of British society which is determined by its own complex historical heritage of diversity. Diversity within culture is inescapable – whoever, for whatever reason, is adding to make it so – because it is living history; and as Jean-Paul Sartre observes, if history seems to escape me it 'is not because I do not make it; it is because the other is making it as well'.[1]

> It is not true that History appears to us an entirely alien force. Each day with our own hands we make it something other than what we believe we are making it, and History, backfiring, makes us other than we believe ourselves to be or to become.[2]

Cultural diversity, such as it is confronted by the writers of this Report, is a managerial formula, an institutional agenda, and, most pertinently, an instrument of governance. Cultural diversity is what happens to culture when it becomes a sector of politics. Someone might justly remark: 'But was it not always so? When has culture not been hostage to the state?' It is not my brief in this introduction to unravel when, how and why things have changed into the recognisably contemporary predicament of culture, indeed a situation that I am tempted to call postcultural. The eight writers contributing to our Report will diagnose the specifics of that cultural condition. I shall limit myself to a few remarks.

The first thing to note is that visual art serves as the Report's reference paradigm. And the reference is chiefly to modernist British art produced after World War II as the example that best illustrates the issue of cultural diversity. Visual art has not been chosen because it is deemed more important than literature, theatre, film, music and dance, but rather because of the peculiarly highlighted position that visual art has come to occupy in the culture market. Contemporary visual art is stalked by a larger number of cultural entrepreneurs and grey eminences than any other art – critics, gallerists, dealers and auctioneers, curators, museum functionaries and so on – and has been swiftly transformed into a global lingua franca advanced by an astounding proliferation of biennales everywhere in the world and often in its least likely corners. No other art is so indissolubly wedded to 'Private Public Partnerships', otherwise said, a Janus interface of the commercial market and publicly funded arts management. The purpose of this suspect union is to instrumentalise art. State cultural policy seeks to gear the arts sector to the Private Public Partnership mechanisms common in the transport and health industries. This is not a collocation resulting merely from fiscal practicalities but a strategic objective of neoliberal governance determined to implement a programme of *equalisation*. We know it flagged by the user-friendly watchwords, social inclusion, popular access, quality of life, accountability and other such desirables in which artists are ensnared by the imperative of civic obligation. Never before have we seen anything so bizarre as the fate of art yoked to reinvigorating the economy and purveying stimulation to the labour market.[3]

This is the predicament in which art finds itself and it parallels that of culture. Awareness of cultural co-option is another reason why art is of special interest to us. Artists were long ago alerted to the snares of instrumentalisation and went through every manner of self-lacerating contortions to 'out' themselves from the clutches of institutions and art market commodification. Conceptual Art seems to me partly explicable as the attempts of artists to turn themselves into escapologists. To no avail. The American critic, activist and curator Lucy Lippard declared 1966 to 1972 the interim period of Conceptual Art in her account of it. Some diffident hope was then invested in Conceptualism's 'dematerialised art', an art idea, as Lippard states, transportable 'in the artist himself' but inapplicable to any art object that travels 'outside him' at the mercy of institutional transactions. But it did not take long for her to see that the hopes in Conceptualism had been largely unfounded.

> It seemed in 1969… that no one, not even a public greedy for novelty, would actually pay money, or much of it, for a Xerox sheet referring to an event past or never directly perceived, a group of photographs documenting an ephemeral situation… a project for work never to be completed… it seemed that these artists would therefore be forcibly freed from the tyranny of a commodity status and market-orientation. Three years later, the major conceptualists are selling work for substantial sums here [in America] and in Europe…[4]

Lippard's disquiet was an early warning of the supra-national culture market expanding at speed into the 1980s and 90s to the present day of recessionary crisis. Gerald Raunig, co-director of eipcp (European Institute for Progressive Culture in Vienna), comments bitterly on the 'perversion of emancipatory practices of the 1970s'. Thereafter the field of cultural policy was opened to 'neoliberal governmentality' in which 'participation is obligatory, creativity becomes an imperative, transparency becomes total surveillance, life-long learning turns into a threat, education means permanent social control, and grassroots democracy means developing software that applicants for cultural funding can use to evaluate each other'.[5] A terrifying indictment of our slippage into an institutionalist mentality. It is surely significant that Ken Kesey's 1962 novel *One Flew Over the Cuckoo's Nest* became a cult classic in the era of 'emancipatory practices' and the film version earned five Oscars in 1975. But the anti-hero of *Cuckoo's Nest* does not escape the long reach of the mental institution. For, just as the ancient Chinese story relates, the monkey cannot jump out of Buddha's hand, so too the artist cannot succeed to evade institutional entrapment. Which does not mean that artists will ever cease striving to do so. The constancy of such endeavours is what dynamically shapes art that probes foresightedly into the future. And this too is the value of art for us: its diagnostic capacity to recognise social failures, as Jean Fisher puts it in her essay, 'often before political culture is aware of them'.

Conceptualism has left us its legacy of institutional critique. The practice of institutional critique was pioneered at the very zenith of Conceptualism by artists themselves. Among them usually credited with its inauguration are Michael Asher, Robert Smithson, Daniel Buren, Hans Haacke, and Marcel Broodthaers.[6] What readers will find in the pages of our Report is a subsequent phase of institutional critique which has reached us in two successive waves, the second coming in the late 1980s into the 1990s, and this *Third Text* Report which itself sits on the crest of a third wave. In that period of forty or so years, institutional critique has percolated diversely through to other workers in the art field, to critics, theorists and curators, and has also become something of an established academic practice. The capillary dispersion of institutional critique was present from the start, going back for instance to the Art Workers' Coalition (AWC), a protest movement in 1969 in America which included Robert Morris, Carl Andre, Hans Haacke, Lucy Lippard and other prominent artists and theorists enlisted from Minimalism and Conceptualism whose '13 Demands' jointly targeted aims for practical artists' rights, museum reform, the representation of women and black artists, and the campaign for cessation of war in Vietnam.

Andrea Fraser, an influential American artist and critic whose career began in the 1980s' second wave of institutional critique, believes that a critical shift to the amalgamation of art and curatorial practices had its start with the AWC in 1969. What began as the AWC's confrontation with the institutional power of MoMA (Museum of Modern Art in New York) and its apparently monolithic façade quickly gained nuance as artists and curatorial staff found common cause in their 'struggles for autonomy from the controlling interests of museum trustees and managers'.[7] Parallel forms of collaboration were emerging at the same time in the work of Lucy Lippard, 'a key member of the AWC who began organising exhibitions of conceptual art almost as early as Seth Siegelaub and Harald Szeeman'. The point is that artistic practices of a conceptual nature and curatorial strategies developed hand in hand but 'from a position that was very critical of museums and galleries, of the market, and the power of trustees and museum managers'. This is what I want to get across – the alignment of neo-avant-garde art with entrepreneurial subsidiary support that might not look like management at all, at first. An uneasy seesaw relationship has prevailed ever since between the aims of artistic autonomy and the sectors of arts administration. It cannot be denied that art is embroiled in the 'culture industry' shaped by the twinning of market forces and state policy, the very essence of neoliberal capitalism, bonded to Private Public Partnerships. Fraser, in the 2005 interview from which I have quoted, asks:

> We've had a hundred years of the avant-garde, we've had forty years of institutional critique – where are we? We're in the midst of the total corporatisation and marketisation of the artistic field and the historic loss of autonomy won over the course of over a century of struggle.[8]

Where indeed are we? I find it telling that in the same year, 2005, Fraser published an article in *Artforum,* 'From the Critique of Institutions to the Institution of Critique', whose title speaks volumes.

> Just as art cannot exist outside the field of art, we cannot exist outside the field of art, at least not as artists, critics, curators, etc. And what we do outside the field, to the extent that it remains outside, can have no effect within it. So if there is no outside for us, it is not because the institution is perfectly closed, or exists as an apparatus in a 'totally administered society', or has grown all-encompassing in size and scope. It is because the institution is inside us, and we can't get outside of ourselves.[9]

To hear this sour note from a long-time activist may be dispiriting; but I think it salutary to take stock of ourselves and reply with considered humility to Fraser's challenge. Is there 'an outside ourselves' from which to gain leverage on institutional closure? Our contributors have not in the least surrendered to pessimism while being perfectly aware that cultural diversity has been in operation almost as long as institutional critique, since 1976, when Naseem Khan's report, *The Arts Britain Ignores,* first offered our cultural institutions an insight into the alienated 'ethnic minorities' of this country. Cultural diversity came to supplant its failed antecedent, multiculturalism, and is proving a more intractable stumbling-block. Did it ever dawn on anyone that multiculturalism was in the first place already a tautological definition of culture? It must be said again and again that 'cultural diversity' as such is not the problem but the policy is that isolates artists of 'diverse cultural backgrounds' in ghettos apart from the mainstream of British art. What happens in the artworld institution is a responsive mirror of what is dramatised in society. Fragmentation, in a word, is what occurs. Deliberate fragmentation which results from a policy of disturbingly near-likeness to cultural apartheid. Diversity is not – and can never be – the same as equality but only a segregationist hindrance to it.

Third Text has been unwavering in its resistance to the separatist agencies of multiculturalism and its cultural diversity metamorphosis. This is largely due to the efforts of Rasheed Araeen, an artist who has certainly never tired of combating artworld institutionalism, who pioneered British Minimalism in the mid-1960s, and since then land and water art, performance art, and so on, and whose origination of *Third Text* twenty-three years ago can be said an art form extended by other means. At the heart of Araeen's discourse in these pages is a clear and simple message that is being ignored and, he would be inclined to argue, wilfully suppressed. It is this. The exclusion of so-called ethnic minority artists from the mainstream British artworld is not and was never the burning issue. Artists of Asian, African Caribbean and African origins were never in need of the dire remedial treatment bestowed on them by a cultural diversity policy that has been anything but benign in diverting attention away from recognition of their decisive role in the modernist avant-garde of post-war British art. The exclusion that cultural diversity perpetrates is that of *not writing them into mainstream art history.* The burning issue is an integral 'whole story' history that can do well by starting with the correction of that exclusion as a first step towards a Britain of truly multicultural heritage for all our benefit. Institutional critique will not progress beyond entrapment in its own ever-proliferating and sterile 'institution of critique' if it does seize hold of art history and (re)write it inclusively.

In my view it is no coincidence that Araeen's independent and long engaged struggle with the artworld establishment echoes that of the Minimalist and Conceptual artists I named earlier as founders of institutional critique. This is because, in his own maverick way, he too inaugurated a potent form of it in Britain. An entire pre-history leading to this *Third Text* Report began in Araeen's four-stage initiatives: the 'Black Manifesto' in 1975–1976; the journal Black Phoenix in 1978; the Black Umbrella organisation in 1984; and Third Text in 1987. Those curious to acquaint themselves with that history should consult the Black Umbrella archive online at www.thirdtext.com.

It must be emphasised however – and Araeen would the first to recognise – that he was not alone in his enterprise but building on another legacy crucially lacking from the phases of institutional critique developed outside Britain. The artists of Asian, African Caribbean and African origins who participated in the creation of avant-garde modernism in postwar Britain by so doing were dealing a death blow to the *institution of Eurocentricity* at the very heart of an exclusionist mainstream. The usual challenge of institutional critique had been aimed at emancipating art from entrapment in managerialism and art market forces, which is undeniably important, but what occurred in British art in the 1950s and 60s took a decisive step towards overturning Western segregationist history and demonstrating the results of artistically productive cultural diversity. 'Look', it is saying to us, 'this is an example of what an integrated society can do.' This uniquely British heritage must not be lost to an ethnically divisive notion of cultural diversity that perverts the future integrated course of creativity.

Is there 'an outside ourselves' that uniquely benefits *Third Text*'s perspective? Of course not. *Third Text* has maintained its critical autonomy in spite of – but admittedly, also because of – funding by the Arts Council and a commercial agreement with Routledge, and is therefore an instance of the Private Public Partnership world in which we live and against which we must resolutely contend.

Our contributors too are each positioned in various degrees of proximity to the central institutional core. (Their biographies are listed at the end of the book.) This is hardly a surprise since the Report is composed by workers in the art, education and administration fields addressing their colleagues in those same precincts, and beyond them to interested members of the public who have no professional link to these sectors. Our common cause is made against the instrumentalisation of culture that reduces it to a corporate service industry.

The handwriting is on the wall, legible to us all at this time of recessionary crisis. Punishing cuts to public sector arts funding on the government's budgetary agenda will undermine the health of British culture not only in the immediate present but for future generations. We are facing what Sir Nicholas Serota, Director of the Tate, has called a 'cultural recession', unmistakably scheduled by the government's plans to 'rescue' the deficit British economy, and we must act at once under inescapable emergency conditions to install new creative partnerships in the public arts sector that are based on a proper understanding and implementation of cultural diversity. But we will not produce such countervailing partnerships unless our efforts are directed by a vision of *cultural solidarity,* that is to say, a socially integrative cultural diversity that severs itself critically, radically and decisively from the past government version.

Action, mobilised by a bold and farsighted partnership programme of cultural diversity, is the underlying message of our Report. We do not seek to impose a monolithic voice on the writers of this Report; but our contributors are all in accord that something must urgently be done to construct a new art history for Britain. Our aim is to achieve what philosophers of science call consilience, a convergence of different sets of facts, drawn together in common pursuit of truth.

There are four main sections to this Report. The first, apart from the Preface by Tony Panayiotou and my Introduction which put the Report in context, includes an introductory essay by Rasheed Araeen, 'Cultural Diversity, Creativity and Modernism', that substantially advances the case for creativity, and it does so on the basis of a genuine, legitimate model of cultural diversity already in practice in Britain over half a century ago but until now ignored. Readers will encounter some British artists either for the first time, or with whom they are insufficiently acquainted, of Asian, African Caribbean and African origins who practised 'cultural diversity' in their contributions to postwar British modernism – but who would never have accepted the terminology of cultural diversity as a true expression of their art.

The Report thereafter falls into two complementary sections. The first in brief provides the reader with an overview of the history of cultural diversity and, as will become clear, that which is is essentially missing from the official and damaging policy of cultural diversity. The section opens with Rasheed Araeen's 'Ethnic Minorities, Multiculturalism and the Celebration of the Postcolonial Other', a passionately articulated experience of being a so-called 'ethnic minority' artist in Britain in the early 1970s. This unhappy experience set him thinking about the deep-structured injustices of exclusion prevailing in the British establishment view of art history that the policies of multiculturalism and cultural diversity have succeeded to disguise ever since the 1970s.

The other contribution to this section by Jean Fisher, Research Associate at Middlesex University and Course Tutor at the Royal College of Art, is an equally impassioned account of cultural diversity in its historical perspective. Her essay, 'Cultural Diversity and Institutional Policy', guides us through a maze of reports on cultural diversity, tracing them from Naseem Khan's classic to UNESCO's 2001 guidelines, among others to date, and exposes their contradictory and often suspect endorsements. She concludes that artistic practices are not reducible to the institutional contexts in which they function.

The next section takes aim at the various flawed aspects of cultural diversity policy that have impacted on community relations in Britain, but also looks ahead with due critical caution to a brighter future for Britain's cultural integration.

The four essays in this section begin with Roshi Naidoo's 'Diversity after Diversity', an uncompromising indictment of the confusions wreaked by cultural diversity that have riven the ethnic communities. Naidoo, an independent Arts and Heritage consultant, provides a welcome and plain-speaking address to sector workers who are often silently frustrated by the top-down policies that they have to implement. Her sensible advice will refresh them in their pursuit of realisable goals.

Victoria Walsh, Head of Public Programmes at Tate Britain, and her co-writers Andrew Dewdney, Professor of Educational Development at London South Bank University, and David Dibosa, curator and researcher at Wimbledon College of Art, have worked jointly through their institutions on a three-year AHRC-funded investigation on cultural diversity. Their essay, 'Cultural Inequality, Multicultural Nationalism and Global Diversity', is a summary of that project and offers some unexpected insights into the hotly contested areas of public access, education and the navigation of postmodern culture.

Art education and art history are two pillars on which to build Britain's new edifice of cultural integration. Leon Wainwright's essay, 'Art (School) Education and Art History', supplies an in-depth review of the troubled mismatch between cultural diversity and art history in this millennium's first decade. Wainwright is a professional educationalist in art history at Manchester Metropolitan University whose findings, extracted from working at the coal face, so to speak, counterpoint Rasheed Araeen's report, 'What is Art Education?', commissioned by the Visual Forum of the Greater London Council (GLC) in 1985. Araeen's report highlighted the disaster that can befall the black art student in the institutional teaching of art history:

> The effect can be illustrated by the experience of a Pakistani artist who was a postgraduate student at the Slade School of Art (University College) in 1956. At that time Professor Ernst Gombrich taught art history there, based on his famous book, *The Story of Art.* He came to a chapter on Islamic art and finished the whole thing in five minutes. His summary dismissal of almost one thousand years of Islamic art had such a shattering effect on Anwar Jalal Shemza, who still lives in Britain, that he went home and destroyed all his work. (Shemza is one of the founders of the modern art movement in Pakistan.)[10]

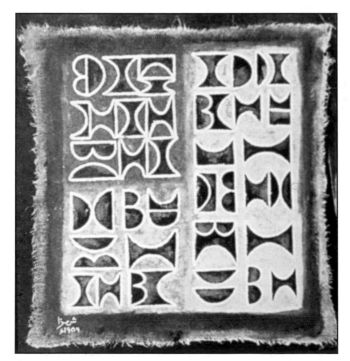

Anwar Jalal Shemza, (b 1928, Simla, India – d 1985, Stafford, England), *The Game*, 1959, oil and tempera, 50 x 62 cm

Araeen's recommendations to the Greater London Council in 1985, never implemented it must be evident, prompt the question: 'What has changed?' Well, one answer is, 'it has become a whole lot more complicated since 1985.' Has it, really? Or is it simple fact that 'what has to be done' has not changed but become hopelessly complexified beyond recognition? Wainwright unravels this incremental 'density' obscuring the issue of art education.

This section closes with a contribution from Hassan Mahamdallie, Senior Strategy Officer, Arts Council of England. His essay, 'Breaking the Code – New Approaches to Diversity and Equality in the Arts', stretches our inquiry beyond the visual art paradigm by visiting other areas of diversity, in particular by instancing the issue of disability and awakening the theatre sector to its long neglect of avant-garde black dramatists.

'Conclusion: What is to be Done?', in the fourth and final section, is a set of propositions in the form of a 10-point programme intended as a platform for research, public debate and a rallying call to all workers in the public arts sector.

I want to end by spelling out the awkward question haunting the writers of this *Third Text* Report. Does anyone know any more what is the use of the word culture? I don't only mean the promiscuous misusage of that word but the obscured extent of its agency. I think one should be wary of the function that culture can serve to disguise from us. Culture is insistently preached as 'good'. Good for what? Good for whom? Whose culture? What exactly are you being sold? Culture is now both a fetish and a commodity, and these two are assimilations of each other, as Marx long ago made clear. Ideology inevitably infringes on culture and contrives it, no matter how 'natural' culture might seem. I would go further and say that whatever is 'naturalised' as a given state of being is in effect ideology. Do we not often see culture reduced to a given state of what is taken for granted – with all its consequent pernicious effects? Culture is nothing of the sort if it succumbs to a nature that exists nowhere but in one's own head.

The vital element of culture is imaginative striving, always dissatisfied with self-justifying complacency; always looking toward being other than one is merely given to be in this lifeworld. Sartre has otherness in aim when he says that our needs, our passions, our most abstract thoughts are *'always outside of themselves toward...'* (his emphasis).[11] Toward what? A project that goes beyond the conditions pre-given to us. Existence does not mean 'a stable substance which rests in itself, but rather a perpetual disequilibrium, a wrenching away from itself with all its body'.[12] What does culture purport, then? 'The world is outside; language and culture are not inside the individual like stamps registered by his nervous system. It is the individual who is inside culture and inside language; that is, inside a special section of the field of instruments.'[13]

If culture is not 'in' us, is not an essentially inhering and restrictive loop from which we cannot escape, then it must have some potentially elective margin of freedom or optative dimension, a 'wish for the Other than oneself', as Sartre puts it. Perhaps a guiding principle can be derived from this idea of freedom. Culture can be judged healthy to the degree in which it permits elective exception to itself, and indeed encourages it to flourish, in the realisation that difference is of indispensable benefit to culture. And culture can best realise its inward diverse potential by interfacing with dissimilar others. Does this actually ever happen? Often, but it is ignored or misconstrued. I think it is the weight of Araeen's argument that the restrictive bonds of one culture can be loosened by creative encounter with another to spark an exceptional freedom of the artistic imagination, as it did with the modernist avant-garde in the first decades of the twentieth century, and as it did again in the 1950s and 1960s of modern British art. This rubbing together of diverse cultures allows the imagination to detach itself from either or any of those cultures and thereby create something new and of beneficial resource to the cultures from which the artist has seemingly floated free. I say seemingly because artistic autonomy can never be supposed absolute. However, the artist's chief constraint is less that of culture than of indebtedness to history, a pact which the artist has no choice but to sign. It should be understood that the artist's agreement with history is not backward looking to the past but a forecasting of the future.

The writers of this Report advocate their 'creative case' on the basis of a forecast future, beyond the conditional terms of cultural diversity, toward a future-shaped hole in the present. And on that basis of futurity the elective emancipation of artistic imagination is an archetype, a motivational pattern, for a truly integrated British society and for the cultural renewal of all humanity. Policy-makers in the arts sector will I hope take enlightenment from this Report to admit the fresh air of future inclusivity into the present.

Ivan Peries, (b 1921, Deriwala, Sri Lanka – d 1988, Southend-on-Sea, England),
Dehiwala, 1978, oil on canvas, 100 x 75 cm

Cultural Diversity, Creativity and Modernism

Rasheed Araeen

INTRODUCTION

An enormous confusion reigns about cultural diversity, which has obscured both the question of its necessity to society and also its relationship to creativity. If human society comprises a multiplicity of diverse cultures, then something must bring them together into a communion of exchange for their mutual enrichment. The history of the last six thousand or so years shows us how humanity has advanced, carrying with it all the ideas produced by the interaction between different cultures within particular civilisations, as well as across those boundaries. It is therefore imperative that we approach the question of cultural diversity historically, in order to understand its significance to the postwar, postcolonial and multi-racial society of Britain today but also globally.

Our concern here is not merely with cultural diversity per se but with its relationship to human creativity, particularly that which produces art. Diversity of cultures and diversity within art must therefore be recognised as two different things, and diversity in art should not be considered necessarily a mirror image of cultural diversity. The passage of diversity from culture to art involves a complex intellectual process which occurs when the individual imagination is relatively free both from the demands of society and the culture of which art is a specific formation and expression. It is therefore requisite to separate the process of creativity from what already exists within society, either as cultural heritage or a multiplicity of cultural traditions. These traditions, of course, define the nature of society and provide it with an overall cultural framework that can be dynamic and inspire individual creativity. But what emerges from this individual creativity as art does not always replicate or display particular cultural forms.

The separation of art from the overall cultural milieu of society does not, however, diminish the importance of the diversity of cultures. They play a fundamental role in defining society and its identity. But if this identity becomes frozen in conformity, society will succumb to cultural fragmentation, intellectual stagnation and eventually decay and decline. Only when people have freedom to think, to reflect and contemplate, can they confront the norms that have become fixed dogmas, and so reactivate society's creative energy. In other words, new ideas produced by individual creativity, underpinned by freedom of thought, create a society able to change and transform itself into a dynamic force in history.

A BRIEF JOURNEY THROUGH HISTORY

Since early history, when human groups began to communicate with each other, diversity has been fundamental to cultures. When two or more cultures met and interacted, inevitably, an interface was created from which emerged a diversity of new cultural forms that enriched the cultures collectively and enhanced individual creative imagination. Out of such imagination, when it was free to think and act, emerged what we now call art.

The increase in travel and speed of communication, facilitated by the rise of modern science and technologies since the Renaissance, has created a constant flow of ideas between peoples, nations and cultures across the world. As ideas often tend to gravitate towards a dominant centre or centres, and since Europe emerged as a major political power following its 'discovery' of the 'New World', knowledge began to accumulate in the major European cities. This accumulation at the beginning of the twentieth century, particularly in Paris, 'capital of the world', is of particular significance. Historically, it laid the foundation for what in my view became essential to the cultural diversity of modernism. Examples abound, Cubism and Surrealism for instance, besides the many individuals whose work was influenced by their admiration of art from Asia, Africa and native cultures of the Americas, proof that the issue of cultural diversity in art cannot be understood without looking at it historically.

Cultural diversity has been very much part of the emergence of new ideas in recent history. Only when this is understood, both in terms of the role of diversity in producing new ideas and of the failure of Eurocentric discourse to recognise the centrality of this role in the art of the twentieth century, will it be possible to reclaim the critical position of cultural diversity within art history beyond the practice of marginalisation on the basis of exotic otherness. We have to make clear the difference between appropriation of other cultures as exotic within Eurocentric art history and their true role in twentieth-century art. While exoticism ignores or undermines this critical role, by banishing it to the margins of history, a proper understanding challenges this marginalisation by invoking and recognising the historically central role of cultural diversity in the formation of modernism at the beginning of the twentieth century.

The very basis of modernism, particularly that which emerged with Pablo Picasso's *Les Demoiselles d'Avignon* in 1907, was an emergence of critical 'dialogue' with cultural difference. Although this dialogue was determined within a colonial frame, the resulting discourse managed to come to terms with what was inevitable at the beginning of the last century: a move away not only from one's own cultural specificity but also from the specificity and the homogeneity of Western traditions in art in order to construct a new order which could claim to be universal.

CULTURAL DIVERSITY AND MODERNISM

The interrelationship of many world cultures in European modernism is extremely complex and problematic. What follows here is intended only to show that it was the presence of cultural forms from other parts of the world entering Europe, particularly in the latter part of the nineteenth century, that, by becoming part of European consciousness, both changed the course of European art and influenced art all over the world. This presence coincided with the discovery of photography which challenged the very foundation of European art. When it became clear that photography could achieve similar and indeed better results than European 'realist' painting had produced, and that there were radical alternatives offered by other cultures, the iconic pictorialism of European traditions in art began to collapse. This created a crisis in what was historically perceived via the idealist philosophy of G W F Hegel, to be the progressive mainstream that began its journey thousands of years before when humans first left their marks on the walls of caves. But with this also arose an awareness that the resolution of this crisis lay in the alternatives offered by other cultures.

If perspectival depth combined with the chiaroscuro technique of a European tradition in art created an illusion of reality, Japanese painting, as it became available to view in nineteenth century Europe, was free of this illusion. This opened up entirely new vistas for European art. Artists now began to realise that art was not only about representing reality through illusionism. There were other different ways of looking at and representing the world.

Until then, the role of line and colour in European art had been to follow faithfully the contours and features of what one observed, so that the result was a representation of what one experienced in nature. If there was an occasional deviation from this norm, it was either to emphasise some important aspects of observed reality or to deal with social disturbances, caused by war or other disasters. Francisco Goya's Black Paintings (1819–1823), made after the upheavals of the Napoleonic War, represent the first example of this deviation in the recent history of Europe, permitting the artist to abandon faithful representation of what one observed. Goya's work, rare in the trajectory of European painting, predates the awareness of the alternatives offered by other cultures some fifty years later, yet foreshadows what became dramatically obvious only when art encountered these alternatives. Line and colour were no longer subservient to the realistic depiction of things but followed whatever the artist could perceive intellectually. This would not have happened without the presence of Asian and African cultural forms in Europe. This shift towards a freedom to perceive and conceive, without recourse to normative realism, was the beginning of modernism in art.

One can cite in particular the late nineteenth-century examples of Paul Gauguin, Vincent van Gogh and Paul Cézanne whose work was transformed when it came into contact with the ideas as well as art forms of non-European cultures, and which then opened the way forward. The role of other cultures in the modern transformation of European art becomes much more determined when we enter the twentieth century. It was the time of great change, with new ideas in science (Aalbert Einstein), music (Claude Debussy followed by Arnold Schoenburg and Igor Stravinsky), philosophy (Henri Bergson), literature (James Joyce, Ezra Pound and T S Eliot), and so on. But my concern here is with visual art, as it was the form most influenced by the presence of many cultures and their art in Europe at the turn of the century.

One might actually describe the beginning of the century as the beginning of cultural diversity, as European culture mingled with many other world cultures. And, although one can begin the century with the art of Henri Matisse, one of the first artists to encounter and become fascinated by African sculpture and whose later work was directly influenced by his visits to North Africa, it was in Pablo Picasso's work that the meeting of Europe and Africa first took place.

At the time, circa 1907, Picasso faced difficulty in continuing his work, as the consciousness of the history in which he found himself located was not only insufficient but had itself become the problem. This is of course over-simplified, but European artists of the time undeniably faced a complex socio-historical situation which they could not resolve within the iconographic realm of Western tradition and still produce something new. It was also a moment significantly reflective of the changes taking place in Western society. It was this situation which led Picasso, among others, to the different world of African and Oceanic art.

When Picasso saw the African and Oceanic artefacts – as they were then called – in the museum at the Trocadéro, he was amazed not only by the freedom of imagination that had created them, but by his own realisation of a potential alternative way of representing the world. Although a radical shift had already taken place in Western art, in the work of the post-Impressionists and Fauves, Picasso's *Les Demoiselles d'Avignon* has been seen as the first real work of twentieth-century modernism. It laid the foundation for Cubism and triggered a historical process based on dialogue between different cultures. When we look at this great painting, *Les Demoiselles d'Avignon,* what do we see? The heritage of Western culture – El Greco, Cézanne, and others – and forms from African and Oceanic cultures, intermingled and interlocked with each other, creating an interface that was to become fundamental to the relationship of different cultures within modernism for the rest of the twentieth century, and also beyond as part of late twentieth century globalisation.

One can also take the work of Matisse and Paul Klee to illustrate the main point, that of a dialogue between the West's iconographic traditions and the Islamic tradition of North Africa. This 'dialogue' is full of problematic, if not unresolved, contradictions – to which I shall return. However, while picture-making dominates their canvases, it is the tension between the iconography of their work and what had been historically in defiance of and a challenge to European pictorialism that makes this work historically significant. This challenge has existed ever since the emergence of an Arab Islamic civilisation and art in the seventh century. But it was dismissed from Europe's historical trajectory as philosophically conceived by Hegel and others. Now, in the early twentieth century, Islamic culture entered into the dynamic force of modernity and began to show a way forward in history.[1] In other words, it was on the basis of modernism's ability to incorporate the problematics of cultural difference within its mainstream that modernism was able to claim its universality, spreading its wings over the whole world and providing the contexts for other cultures to enter into a discourse that claimed progress and advancement.

COLONIALISM AND MODERNISM

I have put the word 'dialogue' in quotes in order to highlight the problem that has remained the basis of a divided world today. Globalisation might seem to reduce division by offering all cultures of the world a common space in which to manifest themselves. This 'equalisation' of cultures is an illusion created by the triumph of the neoliberal/capitalist system whose chief concern is not with the history of ideas and those who have been its agents, but the marketing of commodities. This history has been brought to end with the mistaken notion that what was meant to be achieved historically has been achieved, and that there is nothing further we can learn from it for the future.

What is this history which has 'ended'? Why can it not now be re-examined and revised? Why are art historians reluctant to recognise its missing parts, particularly those which would reveal its cultural diversity? The answers to these questions will reveal the hidden agenda of bourgeois humanism that has been used to justify colonialism, and why globalisation is now being deployed to undermine and 'end' what began as an anti-colonial struggle.

A collusion between modernity and colonialism is well recognised in what is generally called the radical discourse of philosophy and social sciences. Enough philosophical ideas have by now emerged in the West that question the division of humanity on the basis of the Self and the Other – the former being European subjectivity and latter its colonised others. What lies beneath this division is the agency of history attributed exclusively to European (by implication, white) subjectivity, while the colonial other is reduced to the mere victim of history, incapable of self-definition, of determining their destination and entering history. What is remarkable here is not primarily the inferiorisation of the colonised, but that a colonial attitude towards the racially different on the part of the European encompasses an admiration for this difference, and a desire to help and guide them in the march of history.

Colonialism has been and is still a brutal force which dehumanises both the coloniser and the colonised. But it also has a liberal benevolent side which regards the colonised with sympathy and fascination. It has often sided with the colonised and helped them gain postcolonial independence as nation states. But this benevolence does not go far enough, and leaves untouched what is enshrined deep within the ideology of colonialism, failing to allow the colonised to define themselves as free subjects by confronting the so-called master-slave relationship that underpinned colonialism. The slave can demand freedom, and the benevolence of the master can allow the slave to go free; but without the master giving up his own ground.

My concern here is with this benevolent face of colonialism which effectively denies others their human subjectivity, and without which others cannot rid themselves of their Otherness and enter history. This is particularly important when we consider the struggle of art, not only in those areas of the non-European world both during and after the time when these were occupied by the colonial powers, but also in its continuous striving for modern subjectivity in the metropolis. An example from art history will show what I mean. From Matisse to Picasso, Klee and Constantin Brancusi to the Surrealists, each and all were fascinated by the artistic forms of other cultures, especially those of Africa and Asia, and they made these forms part of their work. Some of them even went further in their admiration and expressed their support for and solidarity with the struggles in the colonies. But that is where the solidarity ended, because when they actually encountered someone from the colonies who had come to the metropolis to pursue a course similar to their own as modernist avant-garde artists, there was either suspicion or disbelief that such a person could have ability equal to theirs. Suspicion still prevails, even now that there is overwhelming evidence that others entered the central core of modernism as talented subjects, defying and confronting that which persists in keeping them outside history, and thus demolishing the very basis for white supremacist exclusivity in modern art history. Something deeply entrenched within the European colonial psyche prevents it from recognising equally the intellectual ability of other human beings within modernity.

The dialogue between Europe and the rest of the world has remained problematic to this day. This is not due to the inability of other cultures to find their place subjectively in history or as equal partners in this dialogue. But the space within which 'dialogue' took place was constructed on the basis of a colonial view that divided the world into ruler and ruled, conforming to the Hegelian construct of master-slave relationship, and also apparently fixed this relationship eternally. Master and slave can indeed speak to each other, both have their voices, but only one has significance – that of the master. The master can speak even with the voice of the slave and sympathetically represent the predicament of the slave. But the slave must not claim any subjectivity or agency that might threaten or undermine the power of the master. The struggle of the colonial other is therefore against the supposed benevolence of the colonial master. For if the other were ever to find a place as an obvious agent of history *within* history, this assumption of the benevolent master would collapse, and so liberate the space within which both had been confined in the slave-master relationship.

BENEVOLENT COLONIALISM AND STRUGGLE OF ART

It is important nevertheless to recognise the positive aspects of what I call benevolent colonialism, even when this paradox has collapsed along with the failure of its attempted modernising projects. Whatever it achieved, in its efforts to bring the colonised into the orbit of progressive march of history, has remained contained within the self-interest of colonialism. What concerns me specifically is its educational programme, part of which was to persuade indigenous peoples to adopt Western ways of thinking and living. While missionaries were busy destroying Africa's ancient artistic heritage, often simply burning its artefacts, liberals of the colonial administration encouraged and promoted those who would adopt a Western way of making art. Art schools were set up, particularly in India, and stocked with teachers from the art schools of London. The idea was to lead the native artists on to the path that would eventually lead them to modernism along a track laid down by Europe and the West.

But things do not always go according to a predetermined plan. It is in the nature of humanity not to accept subservience or dominance, not permanently. There comes a time when the oppressed rise up, either to demand equality or to revolt against what is imposed. Many artists confounded the expectations of their patrons and supporters, even when they were genuinely helped in pursuit of their ambitions. There are many instances of artists being sent to the metropolises of London and Paris by their well-wishing colonial patrons. For example, Uzo Egonu from

Nigeria went to London with the assistance of a colonial friend of his father;[2] Aubrey Williams from British Guiana was persuaded by his colonial friends to leave the political turmoil of the country and go to London,[3] and so on. Colonialism was not always a blunt instrument of oppression but frequently provided or created a space in which both the coloniser and the colonised could exist in a mutually sympathetic relationship, giving the colonised the means for the self-realisation of their own humanity, and allowing them to exceed the expectations of their empathetic masters. Behind this paradox lies a deeper unresolvable contradiction, for when the colonised do exceed expectation, sometimes surpassing the ability of the master, what can the master do? Recognise the achievement of the colonised? How can that be? Would it not demolish the very basis of colonial power?

My assertion here may seem crude, but how else can one penetrate the complexity of such an ambivalent relationship and reveal what lies behind it? It involves a sophisticated system that maintains the coloniser and the colonised in mutual dependence and admiration. By invoking the bonds of common humanity, they can even seem to love each other and share each others' pain. But when the colonised try to confront this relationship by asserting their humanity in their own way, this relationship breaks down, often producing the extreme violence that has been a hallmark of anti-colonial struggle.

This relationship had a specific significance in art, particularly during the 1920s and 1930s in Paris when there was great fascination with so-called 'Negro art', described by some historians as Negrophilia.[4] It was during this time that an extraordinary event of historical importance also occurred in Paris, which turned the whole business upside down. Ernest Mancoba, a black South African, set an example of what an individual artistic imagination can do to defy the seductions of colonial predetermination, and offers us allegorically the way forward to the real liberation of humanity. He has shown that the colonised can enter the central core of modernism's genealogy and thereby assert the common humanity of both the coloniser and the colonised.

ERNEST MANCOBA AND THE LIBERATION
OF THE COLONISED IMAGINATION

Ernest Mancoba was born in 1904 near Johannesburg and educated at the Christian school of Pietersburg. He also learned to sculpt there, in a European style, producing a work in 1929 called *Bantu Madonna* which caused a scandal, followed by a series of works that established him as an important sculptor. In 1936 he was offered a lucrative government job but declined it.

> The Commissioner for Native Affairs in Pretoria… decided that I should
> take part in the upcoming British 'Empire Exhibition'. The idea was… to
> develop the indigenous art trade by selling all sorts of pseudo-tribal figures
> for tourists. He offered me a good job with a fine salary, to gather young
> Africans to provide for this kind of traffic. I was shocked and, as politely as
> possible, refused the proposition.[5]

He goes on to elaborate his position:

> Some of my political friends told me that the artistic activity was not the most
> urgent thing to concentrate upon, while our people were undergoing such a
> terrible plight, but I believed, on the contrary, that art was precisely also a
> means to favour a great consciousness in Man, which, for me, is part of the
> struggle for any human liberation, and without which any practical achieve-
> ment would probably, sooner or later, deviate and miss its point. Therefore,
> making art, I thought, was as urgent as for the political evolution, which, at
> the time, anyhow seemed still a faraway prospect. *So I decided to engage
> upon a debate with European artists by coming to Europe.*[6] [my emphasis]

Despite his poverty Mancoba came to Europe:

> As I had absolutely no means to travel, I had the good fortune to be helped
> by missionary institutions, and when I arrived in London, I lived with Bishop
> Smythe, whom I had known as the head of my student hostel at Fort Hare…
> Through Bishop Smythe's connection in Paris, I got into the Ecole des Arts
> Decoratifs.[7]

When Mancoba arrived in Paris in 1938, the city was still in the grip of 'Negrophilia' and the ideas of Negritude.[8] But he turned his back on both of them, with
a defiance that required tremendous courage, leading him to the discovery of the
power of free imagination.

> I suppose I would have managed to understand Césaire and Senghor. But…
> the problem with their approach was that I never believed, for my part, that
> the racist ideology of the Occident is a problem of defective reason or insuf-
> ficient comprehension. And I do not think, therefore, that it can be treated
> by forming new ideological concepts, like Negritude, any more than I would
> imagine that the humanity of the white man might rely upon any virtual
> concept of 'blanchitude'… Because the true universality is a common goal
> on the cultural, political and spiritual horizon that will be reached only when
> all ethnic groups achieve, through an authentic dialogue, the many-faceted
> diamond shape and the full blossom of the deepest and widest human in-
> tegrity.[9]

Ernest Mancoba, (b 1904, Witwatersrand, South Africa –
d 2002, near Paris, France), *Untitled*, 1939, ink and
watercolour on paper, 26.7 x 20.6 cm, courtesy Wonga
Mancoba and Silkeborg Kunstmuseum, Silkeborg

His work of 1939 and 1940 was a precursor to one of the most important postwar
avant-garde movements in Europe, CoBrA.[10] After the war, and his release from
internment, he went to Copenhagen, where in 1948 he met Asger Jorn and Karel
Appel and took part in the Host Exhibition. In the following year, 1949, he became
involved in the founding of CoBrA. But no history of CoBrA mentions Mancoba.[11]
A few years before his death in 2002, Mancoba reminiscenced about his association with CoBrA:

> The embarrassment that my presence caused – to the point of making me, in
> their eyes, some sort of 'Invisible Man' or merely the consort of a European
> woman artist [his wife, Sonja Ferlov] was understandable, as before me,
> there had never been, to my knowledge, any black man taking part in the
> visual arts 'avant-garde' of the Western World… And probably it was also
> our very conception of mankind and of art that not only contributed to our
> isolation from some in the group, but that invalidated us in the appreciation

of the official art world, especially, later, in the eyes and evaluation of certain critics and art historians. Some critics totally obliterate my participation in the movement, as modest as it admittedly has been, on the reason that my work was suspected of not being European enough, and in his words, 'betraying (my) African origins'.[12]

Here is an actual encounter described by Mancoba that demonstrates this attitude:

One day, at the end of 1950s, I met a well-known modern painter of the so-called 'Hard Edge' group. When he saw me together with Sonja Ferlov, addressing both of us, he said: 'Ah, it is you who like the art of negroes [referring to Ferlov's work]. They are full of sensuality, always making sculpture with a big sex, while we modern artists of Europe have left behind these primitive obsessions. Here it is all geometry, purity of lines and clarity of the intellect.[13]

Mancoba's response:

When I tried to tell him that there also was geometry in African art, he shook his head and went away. For me, art can only be founded on the single notion – of which it is both the confirmation and the proof – that Man is One.[14]

Mancoba's work is neither European nor African but in a dialogue with them both. He has created a space in which such a dialogue can and should take place, although this cannot be recognised by the colonial mindset trapped in the power it continues to entertain and enjoy. And thus we have humanity's separation on a racial basis:

...but I'm not thinking about an artistic one. For me, what is still not realised is a common acceptance and understanding between whites and blacks (as the most contrasted opposition in terms of colour, but between other races as well). The dialogue has not started yet. It reminds me of... Danish writer Karen Blixen [when] she says that if the encounter or the meeting between blacks and whites has happened, historically it has, [actually] not yet taken place.[15]

Which brings me to the core of my argument, that the colonised, while struggling to liberate themselves, also liberate the colonisers. Ernest Mancoba's achievement has not only secured his place within the historical genealogy of modernism, but, perhaps more importantly, with this he liberated modernism from its Eurocentric framework *by infusing into its central core an African vision and placing Africa within it with its own authentic modern voice.* It is in such an achievement that there exists, historically, true cultural diversity in art.

AFRICAN AND ASIAN ARTISTS IN POSTWAR BRITAIN

Ernest Mancoba's release from war-time internment in France, and his subsequent extraordinary achievement in art, unprecedented during the classical period of colonialism that produced its most barbaric form in South Africa's apartheid, offers us an appropriate metaphor for the beginning of the collapse of the West's colonial empire and the release of a creativity that enters the European body to liberate it from its self-imposed assumptions of intellectual superiority and supremacy. Surprisingly, even paradoxically, it was a *white* South African in London, Denis Bowen, who recognised this liberated creativity and called it 'a breath of fresh air'. Bowen constantly struggled, along with artists from Asia, Africa and the Caribbean who began to arrive in London soon after the war, against the division of humanity into racial or cultural differences.[16]

However, my concern is primarily with those who faced the problem of being seen, due to their racial difference, as 'others' and who became 'black artists' in the white artworld of Britain. Even when they were right at the centre of modern developments in art, they were seen as merely representing their own Asian, African or Caribbean culture. And with regard to the diversity and experimental nature of the avant-garde activities in 1960s London, Guy Brett has highlighted the problem:

> These qualities have never been recognised by British art history. In fact the entire mainstream historical writing and exhibition-making has been concerned with constructing a national image of British art… ignoring or excluding the work of those foreigners which cannot be assimilated within the national canon. By the cruel logic of chauvinism, official aspirations to make London an international art centre have only resulted in obliterating London's cosmopolitan reality and the actual ferment of its cultural life.[17]

'London's cosmopolitan reality' comprised not just members of the European avant-garde but the active presence of artists of Asian and African origins ('black artists') that turned this reality into a culturally diverse art world. When both white and black artists showed in the same galleries, the basic premises of the modernist avant-garde were transformed into a culturally diverse discourse.[18] Unlike the early part of the twentieth century, when the role of other cultures within modernism was enacted through their cultural objects penetrating into it and precipitating a transformation, now this penetration was that of a *subject* who challenged Eurocentric modernism and liberated it from its white ethnocentrism. When we link this achievement to the exemplary one of Ernest Mancoba, and those of many others in the modern world, we have a completely different history. It is no longer exclusively the history of the achievement of European or Western culture in art

Ethnic Minorities, Multiculturalism and Celebration of the Postcolonial Other

Rasheed Araeen

WELCOME TO BRITAIN

1975 was a watershed in my life. I was forty, had no job and could not earn my living from my chosen discipline, art. Suddenly, one day, I had a strong urge to write. But as an artist I believed my job was only to make art, not to write. I had not learned the discipline of writing, nor was I inclined towards it as a serious means of expression. I had occasionally jotted down my thoughts on paper, but this was something all artists occasionally did without serious concern. But now I had began to feel that there was something I could not express through the artworks I had been making – painting, sculpture, photography, etc. I had to express it in some other way. Maybe writing would help. Why not make the writing a work of art, I thought one day. So I put myself in front of a typewriter and began to strike. My intention was to make an art statement on one A4 page. But once started, I would be with my small typewriter for the next three or four months.

I went through a torturous experience during this period. Although my head was full of ideas, it was extremely difficult to put them down on paper. I had to struggle, often for a whole day, to write a single paragraph that made any sense. But I was determined to see it through, whatever the results. During those months I did nothing but sit at the typewriter from morning to evening, every day of the week. I had no choice but to deal with what was bothering me. I was full of anger and anxiety, not only as an artist but as a human being unhappy with the things happening around me. By the end of this period I had more than one hundred pages in front of me. I put them in a large envelope, and said, 'that's enough'.

It was the end of February 1976 and I became depressed. There wasn't much around to do; or maybe it was the cold weather. I had not been to Pakistan for two years to see my parents. 'Why not go to Pakistan?', I thought. I rang a few travel agents and got a cheap return ticket.

In Karachi I met by chance Mahmood Jamal, whom I had known in London. I gave him the hundred pages that I had typed in London. I was not sure that what I had written made any sense, but Mahmood came back with great enthusiasm: 'You must get it published. It has some grammatical and syntactical problems, but I can help you.' We met again in London on our return, and he helped me with the corrections. I spent another two months re-writing the text. When finished I called it 'Preliminary Notes for a Black Manifesto' and sent it to *Studio International*. A month or so later, I received a telephone call from its editor, Richard Cork, who asked me to come over and see him. When I arrived at his office, Cork looked at me, puzzled: 'I thought you were black'. 'Yes, I am black', I replied and Cork just laughed. The 'Manifesto' was published in 1978. And thus began my involvement in art writing.

The background to this shift from making art objects to writing was a crisis that began in the early 1970s with doubts about what I had been doing as an artist. It was not so much the nature of the work I did as its relationship with the world. How could I carry on making art objects that appeared to have little to do with what was happening in the world? Anyway, nobody wanted to know or understand what I had so far produced as art – even though what I had produced in the 1960s was pioneering Minimalist work in sculpture. How could I expect a system/society to pay attention to the kind of work that was not expected from those who were seen – and are still seen – as 'people from other cultures'? I tried to find answers to these questions by engaging in political activity: first working with the Black Panthers in Brixton, and then with a collective of artists who were engaged in supporting anti-racist and anti-imperialist struggles. This experience of political activity was extremely helpful to me. It clarified a lot of my ideas but did not provide a satisfactory answer to my continuing anxiety about the function of art: how could one make art function as a transformer of society? If art accepted the primacy of political power and was co-opted to the demands of the art market, could it still function as a critical discourse? I realised I could not answer these questions without first examining society and understanding its institutional art system.

It seemed to me that the institutional structures, which defined and legitimised modern avant-garde art practices, were still Eurocentrically trapped in their colonial legacies. It was therefore necessary to re-define the role of art not only to confront these structures, but in so doing also offer a radical alternative in the context of the postcolonial reality of a postwar liberated world.

This search for a different art practice did of course emerge from my own failure and frustration with the artworld. As I was not white and was seen as belonging to a different culture, I realised that its expectations from me were specific and different from what I as a free individual wanted to do as an artist. I always saw

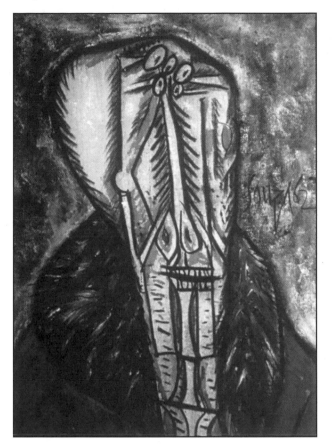

Francis Newton Souza, (b 1924, Goa, India – d 2002, Mumbai, India), *The Manufacturer of Nuclear Weapons*, oil on canvas, 1962

myself as a free human subject of modern history, without necessarily connecting this history to the tradition I was seen to have come from. My interest in art history, particularly in the work of my precursors, therefore led me to probe the official history of art in postwar Britain. But when I began to look into it, I was baffled by the total absence of non-white artists. I knew that many artists of Asian, African and Caribbean origins (henceforth African/Asian or black artists) had been active participants in the postwar British art scene, and the work of some of these artists had been well received and celebrated in the late 1950s and early 1960s. But now they had completely disappeared from the art scene never to reappear either in retrospectives or historical accounts of postwar British art. I was baffled by the total absence of these artists from any debate on or discussion of what constituted the history of art in postwar Britain. I realised that it would be futile for me to carry on producing art when it could not penetrate and be mediated by the culture in which

Avinash Chandra, (b 1931, Simla, India – d 1991, London, England), title unknown, oil on board, c 1964

it was produced, as without this mediation it would not reach its intended audience or achieve its historical significance.

As I began to probe further into the situation and look into the past when black artists were successful, a disturbing picture began to emerge. Although some of them had been highly successful there was something wrong with the way they were received and appreciated. Despite the fact that they produced work as a response to and engagement with modernism in postwar Britain, their work was legitimised differently from that of their white contemporaries. And yet, there was no apparent difference between them: they all showed in the same galleries and were written about in the same magazines and newspapers. They moved in the same social circles and had the same supporters and clientele. But when one looked at the nature of the writing about their work, it was disturbingly different. Artists were differentiated on the basis of their racial differences and cultural backgrounds. Although these writings were often supportive, admiration or appreciation was underpinned by a gaze that turned these artists of African or Asian origins into primitive or oriental Others. This was not very different from how black people were in general being treated. Racial and cultural differences between white and black peoples were constantly invoked to determine their social status – both positive and negative – in British society.

When peoples from the Caribbean and the Indian subcontinent arrived in Britain in the early 1950s, they were at first welcomed. They had to be, as they were desperately needed workers for the postwar reconstruction of British industry and infrastructure of transport, communication and other social services. The situation for artists from Asia, the Caribbean or Africa was somewhat different. Their role was not yet defined. In the beginning, they had to struggle hard in order to find a place in British society; and, by the end of 1950s, some of them had succeeded. They were enthusiastically welcomed into the mainstream artworld and some became well established.

While the workers helped restore British economic life to normality, indeed set it on a prosperous course that led to the optimism and cultural blossoming of the 1960s, African/Asian artists turned London into a cosmopolitan multiracial art scene. But this was not to last very long. By the mid-1960s, even the successful artists began to feel that things were changing. In fact, as the fascination with the exotic Others faded, they began to be disregarded and eventually disowned. It was therefore no surprise that Francis N Souza, Iqbal Geoffrey, Avinash Chandra and Frank Bowling saw no future in Britain; they packed up and left for New York. The workers also began to realise that they were being exploited by being railroaded into menial work. Even when they were qualified to do better jobs, their wages were much lower than those of white workers doing the same job; and the accommodation available to them was only run-down houses without basic amenities. When they started protesting about these conditions, they were seen as a problem.

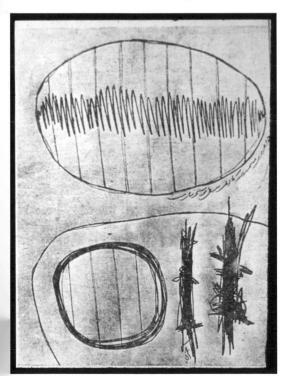

Iqbal Geoffrey, (b 1939, Chiniot, Pakistan), *In Search of an Ideal Landscape*, c 1960s, from a series of twenty-two paintings on paper

THE YEAR 2005

Years later, in 2005, I find many people in a state of multicultural euphoria. Things have indeed changed, in some respects so much that it is no longer easy to criticise the system. The racism of British society is now openly recognised and the government has put forward many schemes to deal with it.[1] The system is

Aubrey Williams, (b 1926, Georgetown, Guyana – d 1990, London), *Hymn to the Sun IV*, 1984, oil on canvas

spending millions of pounds in support of cultural diversity, with African/Asian officers placed in local councils to look after the cultural interests of their respective so-called 'ethnic minorities'. We now also have some representatives in Parliament as well as in the House of Lords; and those who are considered to have exceptional achievements to their credit are being rewarded with OBEs and MBEs.

With the emergence of multiculturalism in the late 1980s, the artworld also opened its doors again to black artists. Today the British art scene includes many such successful and celebrated artists. In the 1950s and 1960s the success of the earlier generation of black artists had been limited. It did not go much beyond British shores, and when some of them went to New York, following the general trend, they did not succeed there. In comparison the present generation is doing extremely well. In the past they would not have been celebrated by a retrospective at the Hayward Gallery or expected to win the Turner Prize.

However, not all artists left for New York. In fact, a period between the mid-1960s and late 1970s was very important for those who remained in Britain and were involved in the forefront of the avant-garde – and some still are. But their presence was totally ignored by the art establishment. In the early 1980s, things began to change, not in favour of these artists – whose pioneering work is still institutionally disregarded – but for the younger generation.

The success of the younger generation of artists is, it seems, part and parcel of the emergence of multiculturalism, as what is produced by them is culturally specific. Let us be clear. This is specificity only meant for those who are considered 'others', and hence the colonialist separation between people based on racial or cultural differences has now been, I would argue, openly institutionalised and maintained. And this 'cultural specificity' has also helped the institutions to displace the critical and subversive position of the work of earlier generations.

Why and how has all this change come about? Two facts have interlocked and conspired in producing a supposed change. I aim to explore and deal with this question both historically and ideologically. I will highlight the historical nature of the struggle specifically in visual art, but also what emerged politically and socially in

Uzo Egonu, (b 1931, Onitsha, Nigeria – d 1996, London, England), *Restaurant at Bad Orb*, 1980, oil on canvas, 124 x 178 cm

parallel to this struggle, and their interconnections. The struggle for the recognition of Britain's black or African/Asian artists was not an isolated struggle within the artworld. There were also other struggles outside, both in political and cultural arenas, which together played highly complex and contradictory roles. While the socio-political and cultural struggles in general had created an awareness of the need for this society to recognise its postwar multicultural reality, these struggles somehow failed to confront the institutions with their failure to acknowledge what had been the historical achievement of all people in art within mainstream modernist developments. What we see as change today has occurred not as a result of awareness or desire for change, following external or internal criticisms, but only as a response to socio-political pressures from the so-called 'ethnic minority' leadership. The art establishment had no choice but to respond to these pressures, as things had begun to get out of hand, and the result was multiculturalism or cultural diversity. This got the system off the hook, as a change of this sort could be brought about without confronting or challenging its basic institutional structures.

A second factor to recognise is that multiculturalism is a broad cultural phenomenon resulting from the genuine desire of the immigrant communities to maintain their own cultural roots and assert themselves culturally through these forms. But this has played into the hands of the establishment as a means to impose its own agenda of cultural diversity, which would end not in the recognition of the historical struggles of African/Asian people in Britain for equality but in the emergence of cultural spectacles whose purpose is merely to provide exotic entertainment.

This shift from initial critical engagement with society to the present multicultural entertainment industry has not happened suddenly but through a gradual process which involved the artistic as well as socio-political struggles of these 'ethnic minority' peoples. Their initial welcome into postwar reconstruction faded as Britain recovered its economic self-confidence and voices hostile to immigrants began to be heard. This, in my view, affected the status of African/Asian artists and contributed to their disappearance from the British art scene.

We cannot begin to understand this complex socio-economic phenomenon, which has affected two generations of British artists of all 'ethnic' origins, without grasping the nature and ideology of the neoliberal worldview for which the value of every human effort is measured by its success in the market place.

WHEN THE IMPERIAL LION ROARS
In 1968 Enoch Powell, a highly respectable and respected parliamentarian, delivered his famous 'Rivers of Blood' speech in which he proposed the expulsion of those he considered new immigrants arrived from the British Commonwealth. Perhaps there is no direct connection between Powell's speech and how black art-

ists have been subsequently treated, but his views are important in understanding the perception of 'other' artists in Britain, as well as in the West as a whole. Powell had persistently maintained that he was not racist but was only concerned with what was happening to Britain as a result of postwar immigration. The new immigrants were disturbing the established order by changing the character of British society and its culture, and for him this change was unacceptable. However, he would be happy with a small manageable minority, which kept to its own affairs and did not intervene or interfere with the values of the white mainstream culture. He also in his subsequent statements maintained that African and Asian people could never belong here because they were of different racial and cultural stocks.

Powell's view represents two things: a) African/Asian people do not belong to British society but a small 'manageable' number of them can be accepted to perform specific jobs; b) they cannot and should not be allowed to penetrate and disturb the established order of British society. This view is not just Mr Powell's, but is a foundation of British institutions and indeed of the West as a whole, by which those who are not of European racial origins are constantly marginalised by relegating them to culturally defined manageable minorities.

It is interesting to remember that Mr Powell was himself responsible for persuading peoples from the Caribbean and the Indian subcontinent to come to Britain as labour recruits. There is a striking analogy here. Just as cheap labour, once used, was cast aside, so also artists no longer required to give exotic colour to the British art scene were ignored.

What happened in the British art scene subsequent to Mr Powell's speech? In 1972 there was an important show of 'New Art' at the Hayward Gallery representing decisive conceptual shifts and breakthroughs in art in the second half of 1960s. It was meant to canonise certain artists and secure their place in history, but, not surprisingly, all the artists included in the show were white. Even an artist like David Medalla, for example, whose avant-garde activities were well known and whose ideas had influenced some of the artists in the show, was excluded. The art critic Rosetta Brooks has recently recognised Medalla's influence:

> His project... anticipated both American and British land art by nearly a decade. Medalla's art was a challenge to that cut-off of the fragmentary commodity which formalism created out of the art work. His works were too cosmic, too political, and too all-inclusive to submit to commodifying fragmentation. For Medalla, the art work was an opportunity to communicate rather than an opportunity to fall into reverential silence.[2]

In 1963, Medalla began to make his kinetic sculptures in which he used commonplace materials like liquid soap, sand or mud, much before similar materials

David Medalla, (b 1942 Manila, Philippines), *Cloud Canyons no 2*, 1964,
ensemble of bubble machines, London, collection of the artist, photo: Clay Perry

became the hallmark of Arte Povera. In 1964 he published a series of proposals for conceptual work, such as walking, sleeping, panting and singing sculptures.[3] In 1967, he gave up making art individually in favour of working collectively with poets, musicians, dancers, singers and others in what he called the 'Exploding Galaxy'. His pioneering and revolutionary ideas had tremendous impact on some, albeit reactionary, British artists who were hailed as innovators in the 'New Art' show. One can think of the celebrated walks of Richard Long, and the singing sculpture of Gilbert and George.

Medalla's exclusion from this historical exhibition was by no means an unusual occurrence. It had happened to many African/Asian artists before and continues to happen even today. The 1976 exhibition in Milan, 'Arte Inglese Oggi: 1960–76' (English Art Today: 1960–76) selected by the British Council, representing all the developments that had taken place since the 1960s, included more than sixty artists – but none of them was an African or Asian. Even those African and Asian artists who had been highly successful and celebrated in the 1960s were not there. This happened again in the big Paris retrospective of British art in 1979 'Un Certain Art Anglais' (A Certain English Art); and the story is endless. The point I am emphasising is that artists of African/Asian origin were not altogether neglected or ignored, but none were considered when it came to defining and constructing the genealogy of the history of modern art and its various developments. This amazing anomaly is not at all amazing when we appreciate that history is not necessarily an objective account of facts but is ideologically constructed and upheld by its ideological players.

It is hardly enough to invoke Mr Powell's explicit and transparent views to understand why these artists could not be part of British history. The underlying ideas are much more complex and operate subtly through sophisticated art institutions. They can, and often do, transcend the ideological distinction between right and left. Powell's speech did of course have much more visible and direct repercussions on the general situation of African/Asian people in Britain than anything that happened to artists. Following his speech, many white workers came out on the streets in support of his position, and right-wing fascist organisations emerged whose young followers became known as 'skinheads', notorious for their racist violence.

Powell's speech also had further historical significance. It coincided with a shift to the right in British politics, a reaction to the growing radicalisation not only of politics but of culture. The end of the sixties was an intense political period, characterised by student uprisings in Paris and elsewhere, growing worldwide opposition to the war in Vietnam and solidarity with anti-imperialist struggles. Many radical African/Asian organisations were also created to mobilise their communities and demand an end to racism and secure equality for all citizens. Some artists also joined in this struggle, which led to the formation of 'Artists for Democracy' in 1974, and helped to politicise many artists in favour of anti-racist and anti-imperialist struggles.

RETURN OF THE COLONIAL OTHER

These radical developments and growing militancy among the non-white population faced the establishment with a difficult situation. What could be done about it? The problem was how to avoid doing anything that could create a further threat to its established order. A solution had to be found that would appear to offer something positive, but in reality would diffuse and displace these escalating radical demands. If the establishment could find some African/Asians to co-operate in this respect, it could do the trick. So began the lure of cultural funding.

In 1973, the Gulbenkian Foundation invited some people from the African/Asian communities to a one-day conference to discuss what was described as the 'black problem'. But radical black groups, knowing what was on the agenda, boycotted the conference. We do not know exactly what was decided at the conference, but, given that the Gulbenkian Foundation is a cultural organisation, the conclusion must be obvious. It must have been about culture and its role in community relations.

Following this, a journalist, Naseem Khan, was commissioned by the Gulbenkian Foundation, with backing from the Arts Council and the Community Relations Commission, to investigate the matter. After two years' research, Naseem Khan produced a report, *The Arts Britain Ignores: The Arts of Ethnic Minorities in Britain.*[4] The report's conclusion was that the so-called minorities had their own traditional cultural forms, and these forms had been ignored. And that is why black people felt excluded from mainstream British society. In order to make these minorities feel at home in Britain, they must be encouraged to develop and express themselves through these forms.

As far as I remember, it was the first time that I came across the word 'ethnic' to describe African and Asian communities, and with this emerged the so-called 'ethnic minority arts'. Nothing much happened immediately, but it did lay the foundation for what was to become a minority discourse separated from the majority mainstream context. Similar things occurred at the same time in other parts of the Western world wherever there was a significant non-white population, particularly in Canada and the US, which eventually led to what we know today as multiculturalism.

While the art establishment was considering the demands for 'ethnic minority arts' funding, another politician unleashed her racist demagoguery against immigration, some ten years after Mr Powell's vicious speech which 'had erupted' in white violence against black people. Now it was the turn of an ambitious Tory politician who aimed to be Prime Minister. In fact, without that 1979 speech, in which she irresponsibly aroused the fear of the white population against others by saying that 'this country might be swamped by people of a different culture', Margaret Thatcher might not perhaps have won the election.

While some politicians turned the presence of black people in Britain into a political issue, in order to stir public opinion against them, the liberal section of society tried to calm the whole thing down and thereby provide a cover for it. But liberalism's carrot of 'altruism' did not arrive in time. With the victory of Mrs Thatcher, it was no longer possible for black people in the 1980s to tolerate their degradation and contain their anger and frustration, and there followed what the media described as 'black riots' in the major cities of Britain. When the repressed returned with a vengeance, it became clear to the political establishment that it was not dealing with a docile minority. What it faced was fire with which it could not continue to play without dire social consequences. Something had to be done to contain the growing rebellion of the African/Asian youth. Following these uprisings and riots, the Thatcher government, which was in the first place responsible for them, appointed Lord Scarman to investigate the matter.

Lord Scarman, who spent considerable time consulting the emerging black community leadership, reached the conclusion that there was 'cultural alienation' among the black youth. His report recommended that the Government fund art and cultural projects in areas with large non-white communities. In fact the Arts Council had by then, in 1982, already issued a press release entitled 'Arts Council to encourage ethnic arts', in which it announced its intention 'to incorporate the needs of the ethnic arts as a specific element in its submission to the Government for 1983/84'.[5]

Mrs Thatcher's reign produced a general revolt against the Conservative Party that led to the Labour Party's massive victory in London's local elections and the takeover of the Greater London Council, under the leadership of Ken Livingstone, with a specific programme of funding the cultural activities of what was officially described as 'ethnic minorities'. Although the GLC did not last very long, it left a legacy which gave people an awareness of their power to demand their cultural rights. After the abolition of the GLC in 1986, the Thatcher government found itself in a 'multicultural' situation it could not ignore; and not surprisingly it instructed the Arts Council to spend four per cent of its budget in that direction. What shall we call this? A paradox, an about turn, or a political strategy to appease or subdue dissidence? How was it that the very same Mrs Thatcher who won the election by inspiring fear in Britain of 'people of a different culture' was now prepared to give government support and funding to promote the cultures of the same people? The media also moved in and Channel 4 created a special fund for 'ethnic minority' programmes. All this concern for 'immigrants' sprang not from a sudden love of their cultures, or an attempt to understand the real significance of what they could contribute in transforming society into an integrated multicultural society. It was rather a farsighted cultural strategy to produce a class of ethnic functionaries that would assist in containing the radical demands of a disenfranchised people for full equality in every section and level of the society to which they had made a great contribution.

However, this official policy of supporting and funding 'ethnic minority arts', on the basis of different and specific cultural traditions of different people, gave rise to further social problems with all their ideological implications. But before I go further into this, it would be useful to clarify the complex position that cultural traditions occupy in a modern society, particularly when cultural traditions migrate from their roots to a new habitat in a foreign country.

When people migrate, they carry with them their own cultures, with their forms and values; and when people are confronted with a hostile or an un-inviting host population, their own cultures can provide comfort. Culture in this instance can provide shelter against what is unpleasant and also compensate for what one is not able to achieve in the new country. It is the right of all people to maintain themselves within their own cultures, wherever they are, and it is also their right to protect their cultures, their creative forms and values. In this respect I have no problem with traditional cultures and it should not be an issue.

However one cannot fail to recognise that there are cultural forms produced by feudal, monarchic and theocratic systems. They have their historical value and importance, but when these forms are revived uncritically to give a particular society or community its contemporary identity on the basis of its past achievement or nostalgia, they do not offer a way forward. Rather, they function regressively by stifling or diverting the creative imagination away from contemporary reality. My concern here is particularly with art and its role in our modern culture. The critical function of this role is often subverted by containing it within the forms that belong to some remote past.

So also we should distinguish between nostalgic desire for old cultures and a cultural resistance in which indigenous traditions can play an important role. An oppressed old culture can rejuvenate itself when it becomes part of a struggle against the oppressor or an oppressive system. But the role of traditional cultures in multiculturalism is entirely different. It is now used to define the social role of those who are considered 'others' in contemporary Western societies, to camouflage their real deprivation, and to displace and subvert their growing opposition to what has now become a global system of exploitation and plunder.

BLACK ART AS RESISTANCE

The emergence of the idea of 'ethnic arts' in the late 1970s did not go unquestioned. Many were swift to realise that there was something insidious behind the establishment's concern for 'ethnic' cultures; it was particularly felt by some artists that they were being ethnicised in order to marginalise them further. I myself wrote a critique of it, soon after Naseem Khan's report came out in 1976.[6]

In 1978, I started an art magazine, *Black Phoenix*. Its first issue contained my 'Black Manifesto',[7] but it was also meant to give voice to those who were critical of a perceived subtle form of cultural apartheid. It provided a platform to debate and analyse what was happening in art, not only in Britain but globally. Our position regarding the status quo was very clear. Our position as artists was at once specific but also part of the overall struggle against cultural imperialism. We did not separate the struggle in art from the socio-economic and political realities.

One of the most important developments of the early 1980s was the emergence of what its protagonists called 'Black Art'. It was not a name given to anything that might be produced as art by black people, but to the specific work done by a group of young black artists in opposition to the prevailing order. This group, whose main figures were Eddie Chambers and Keith Piper, both born in Britain of African-Caribbean parents, not only accused the system of institutional racism but wanted to make art that confronted racism and imperialism. Their ultimate aim was to make art for the black community as a weapon of resistance in Britain and globally. They called for the unity of African people all over the world against the oppressive forces of imperialism.[8]

This laid the foundation of what became known in the 1980s as the 'Black Arts Movement', which drew in many young black art students, and was an impetus for a debate critical of the system. Art institutions were accused of deliberately ignoring and suppressing the history of African/Asian artists in Britain. And that was something the promoters of 'ethnic arts' did not talk about but rather seemed to collude with the establishment in suppressing and undermining. However, as the establishment's own agenda of 'ethnic arts' began to gain popular support among the deprived classes, for whom something was better than nothing, the 'Black Arts Movement' was subverted. There were enough people happy to be part of the system.

ESTABLISHING ETHNICITY IN ART

At the end of the 1970s, exactly when this critical debate was going on, a young Indian man finished his postgraduate course at Chelsea College of Art. He visited

India after leaving college. There he saw piles of colourful spices being displayed in bazaars in the form of conical shapes placed on the ground. On his return to London, he made similar shapes with powder pigments in dazzling bright red, yellow, blue and other colours, and immediately got a gallery to show them. Soon after, Anish Kapoor was the talk of the artworld.

In 1982, something else extraordinary happened that seemed to pave the way for Kapoor's successful career. It was the grand 'Arts of India' festival which occupied almost every major gallery and museum in London. Another paradox? Why would a right-wing Conservative government be interested in the arts of India? Was it another means of appeasing the Indian community in Britain? Of course, the festival was used as an exercise in community relations, but was there not a hidden agenda of far more importance? The festival did attract the interest of a large number of people from the subcontinent, but it had another aim. Did not Britain subsequently gain a profitable contract with India to supply her with advanced military hardware, among other things?

Whatever the real motives behind the festival, it was undoubtedly an impressive event. It provided an opportunity to see the cultural richness of Indian civilisation, going back to ancient Vedic times. It happened also in the wake of Salman Rushdie's successful novel, *Midnight's Children,* for which he won the Booker Prize in 1981. Although a brilliant work, it was a nostalgic look at India as a faraway exotic place. The media was already in a state of obsessive celebration of Rushdie's fantastic India when the Indian festival opened in the spring of 1982, fuelling more public fascination with everything Indian. It was in some way a déjà-vu – a return to the Maharishi of the 1960s hippy period.

In the same year, Whitechapel Art Gallery held an important show, 'British Sculpture in the Twentieth Century', which included all the figures that the establishment considered to be historically relevant. Nobody expected this show to include an African/Asian artist, but, to everyone's surprise, Anish Kapoor appeared in the second part. It was a surprise because Kapoor was a newcomer to the art scene. It was yet to be seen whether he would achieve anything historically significant that would make him eligible to stand amongst the prestigious British sculptors of the twentieth century. He was not on the list of the artists the gallery had issued before the exhibition, nor was he mentioned in the catalogue. The decision to include Kapoor in the show seems to have been a last minute one, the logic of which might elude us. But it does have a logic that we will presently unfold. Following this show, he was taken up by the Lisson Gallery, and is now one of the most celebrated artists in the UK and world-wide.

I am not objecting to the inclusion of Kapoor in the Whitechapel show or to his subsequent promotion by the art establishment. But there seems to me clear

Kim Lim, (b 1936, Singapore – d 1997, London, England), *Day*, 1966, painted steel, 214 cm high

ideological motives for this, other than those by which important artworks tend to be recognised. For this was the moment when the issue of the exclusion of Africa/Asian artists from art history had become public knowledge and was being publicly debated. Kapoor's arrival on the scene, with his Indian exoticism, helped the establishment to defuse the controversy. Kapoor is an intelligent and imaginative artist, and he has every right, like any other artist, to pursue a successful career. That is not the point. The issue is the nature of the role bestowed on him, whatever and apart from the genuine merits of his work, and what this signified in the early 1980s, and subsequently, when the system was confronted with the demand for a radical change in its institutional structures. He appeared in the establishment's view to conform to the notion that the work of non-white artists is authentic only when it makes a connection with their African or Asian cultures. Kapoor was the opportunity needed by which the system could make plain what it specifically expected from African/Asian artists in Britain. They would not easily obtain recognition unless their works showed their African or Asian credentials, related only to their own cultural conditions of being.

Other black artists, who had enjoyed success in the early 1960s, owed it to the establishment's discovery and celebration of some traces of 'African/Asian cultures' in their works. Judging by the success of Kapoor, and of many others since, as a result of their use of their 'ethnic' cultural identities in their work, the whole thing has come full circle.

RETURN OF THE COLONIAL

The colonial system has always responded to the demand of the colonised for equality by diverting their attention to their own traditional systems. When at the end of nineteenth century India's Westernised middle-classes demanded self-rule, it was seen by the colonial rulers as a dangerous consequence of modernity. They then tried to persuade this class to give up Western ideas and look to their ancient cultures for the solution to contemporary problems. In art this happened when the Englishman E B Havell became principal of the Government School of Art, Calcutta, in 1896. Havell realised that the British Empire was at risk because the Westernised Indians had begun to aspire to the Western liberal system and its humanist values – ironically, introduced there to educate and civilise the Indians – and were demanding that the system put in practice what it was teaching. He immediately put a stop to all modern methods of teaching and sent his students to study the ancient Vedic texts.[9]

A section of the 'native' middle-class intermediaries, by seeking to accommodate itself to the imperial structure through increasing participation in the economy and administration of the colony on the basis of equality, may eventually pose a threat to the colonial mode of production and administration. When this happens, as it did towards the end of nineteenth century, with persistent middle-class demands for modernisation, imperialism turns to the anti-modernity traditionalists. Hitherto opposed to imperialism because of the threat it posed to pre-modern institutions, the traditionalists now become imperialism's natural ally against their common enemy – the modernising middle-class. Havell appealed to the imperial masters in London by saying: 'In honouring the Indo-Aryan forerunners of India, we shall honour ourselves and make the most direct and effective appeal to Indian loyalty'.[10]

Anish Kapoor's success, like that of his African American contemporary Jean-Michel Basquiat in the US, marked the beginning of the cultural phenomenon from which emerged a postcolonial Other. This new Other enters into the Western system of modernity through the backdoor of postmodernism, not inferiorised or degraded this time but celebrated as an expression of the benevolent multiculturalism of Western societies. With all due respect to Kapoor, I could not overlook his declaration that there was no such thing as racism in art. When I reprimanded him for this, he wrote to me: 'I... feel that the most effective way of combating racism is by way of making an art which is rigorously Indian and not by political action.'[11]

In 1989, I organised 'The Other Story' exhibition at the Hayward Gallery, in which the history of art produced by African/Asian artists in Britain was put on display so that the public could see for themselves the achievement of multiracial Britain.[12] The show was received enthusiastically by the public, but the art institution as usual displayed an indifference which even to this day remains the hallmark of the institutional attitude. Kapoor was invited to take part in this exhibition, but he declined – which was of course his prerogative. The opening of his own show at the Lisson Gallery in the same week as 'The Other Story' gave the media an opportunity to rubbish 'The Other Story' and dismiss any suggestion of racism in the artworld.

MODERNISM AND THE OTHER

It is now believed by some, if not indeed many, from the so-called 'Third World' that to pursue a course within the historical trajectory of modernism amounts to mimicry of Western culture. This, in my view, is based on a simplistic reading of some ideas in Western philosophy going back to Immanuel Kant and G W F Hegel. Of course, there are many disturbing contradictions in this discourse, with pernicious racism hidden behind its Eurocentricity, but this philosophy also provides the means to overcome these contradictions and possibly resolve them. Rejection of modernism also means rejecting the Hegelian-Marxist tradition which lays down the basic framework of the dialectics of struggle for universal liberation. If there are now problems with this tradition, it not only has to do with its prevailing Eurocentricity but also with how Eurocentricity constructed the framework and narratives of modern art history.

The history of modernism is a history of colonial discourse, the logic of which demands that it construct and maintain Eurocentric narratives. But what purpose do these narratives serve when their underpinnings have collapsed with the end of colonialism? The obvious answer would be to assume that what was a manifestation of colonialism should have ended with the end of colonialism. But how would one then explain why the history of modern art in the twentieth century is still the exclusive history of white European and North American artists?

I have been asking this question for more than two decades, but no one within the established order seems concerned with it. It is either dismissed as irrelevant or sometimes elicits the sort of sympathy that assumes the inability of African/Asian Others to enter the modernist discourse and prove their worth. This assumption is entrenched in the Eurocentric ideology of modernism. But why does this assumption persist without being tested rationally against the facts that apply to a critical discourse on the assessment and legitimation of art? Modernity has emerged from and is defined by Europe and cannot therefore be anything but Eurocentric. But what lies masked behind Eurocentricity is not simply the fact that Europe has been

Li Yuan Chia, (b 1929, Lushan, China – d 1994, Carlisle), *Floating Disc Toy*, 1968–1969, twelve metal painted discs, each 90 cm in diameter, installation at 'The Other Story', Hayward Gallery, 1989

the centre of the world since its ascendancy five hundred years ago, but how this centre is defined and constructed. This centre is maintained as the exclusive domain of the 'master' and the rest of the world as that of the 'subalterns'. This relationship between the centre and what surrounds it peripherally is then reinforced racially. Upon this relationship a philosophy of (art) history has been constructed, the agency of which is attributed exclusively to the white subject. For Hegel, the dynamic of history – and the very ability to move forward with new ideas – is dependent on a human agency that has the freedom to define itself and others. But the subaltern or the colonised cannot be the agent of history.

Therefore, since the philosophy of (art) history is constructed in the language of modernity, should this language not be the centre of struggle? If this language is the language of domination, then the struggle of the 'other' would be to seize it and turn it against domination. Although all artists who pursue radical alternatives to what is already legitimised by the institutions have to struggle to find something new to enter modernism's history, the struggle I refer to has an additional dimension. While pursuing what is taken for granted by white artists – their place in history

– black artists have constantly to struggle against this taken-for-granted position. Euro-ethnocentricity continues to define and determine the still prevalent historical framework of modernism in which racism in art resides. Behind this lurks the perpetuation of the colonial myth of white intellectual supremacy – but precisely this linkage of presumed supremacy has been debunked by the pioneering avant-garde works of some African/Asian artists in Britain.

The achievement of an earlier generation of 'other' artists was not merely that they managed to penetrate the citadel of modernism and claim their place in it as free subjects. They also challenged its prevailing ideology and redefined modernism beyond its Euro-ethnocentric premise; and by so doing they expanded its premise, so that it became an expression of the freedom of all peoples from all cultures. This was part of the critical process to move the colonialist society on to its next historical phase, to help it decolonise itself and its institutions, so that it could recognise the equality of all its citizens without relegating some to the status of 'ethnic minorities'. African/Asian modernists were not unusual in following the avant-garde creed of challenging the established order of things. But what

Rasheed Araeen, (b 1935, Karachi Pakistan) installation at 'The Other Story', Hayward Gallery, 1989; on wall, left: *8bS,* 1970, painted wood, 183 x 394 x 38 cm; right: *Green Painting,* 1985–1986, mixed media, 173 x 226 cm, Arts Council Collection; on floor, part of *Chakras,* 1969–1970, sixteen waterdiscs, each 61 cm in diameter; to right: *Sculpture no 1,* 1965, 30.5 x 183 x 183 cm

was unusual was that this time a new challenge came from those defined by the dominant ideology as the Other, from those considered peripheral to this modernist tradition. One should not be surprised that this challenge was sidelined, and with it an important part of postwar history.

There is now an alarmingly irrational tendency to declare that all modernist and avant-garde works of 'other' artists are derivative because influenced by what is said to be Western modernism. If we accept this argument, then we must declare most of the works in the history of modernism equally inauthentic, influenced as they were by other cultures. There is no point in contesting this feeble and facile argument. What is imperative is to look at what differentiates two similar works which have been produced during the same time and are the products of the same historical process. Why are some works evaluated on basis of their unimpeachable modernity and canonised, while similar works produced by 'other' artists are subjected to racial or cultural differentiation?

We do not yet have a proper theoretical or philosophical discourse vis-à-vis art history that is able to criticise modernism's hidden Euro-ethnocentricity so that it can open the doors of modernism to all, irrespective of racial or cultural differences.

THE SPECTACLE OF MULTICULTURALISM

Producers of art of whatever ethnic origin in contemporary culture must be free from any predetermining perceptions and constraints of specific cultures. To force individual artists into a predetermined cultural territory is similar to what apartheid did to black artists in South Africa. The success of a few black artists today should not disguise the fact that behind their success lies a discourse of discrimination. Apartheid is apartheid even when it operates benevolently towards those who are deprived and oppressed. Such an institutional strategy could only succeed because enough people, including artists, were ready to oblige. The basic objective of this strategy was to safeguard the white genealogy of modern art history from the contamination of the 'other' by locating the 'other' artists somewhere else and in such a way that they would not demand a place in what they themselves had denounced as Eurocentric. This strategy has now become so successful that no international exhibition today can afford to be without African/Asian artists, either from the metropolis or mainland Africa or Asia. The success of a number of these artists today becomes an alibi in the neglect and suppression of earlier works which questioned and challenged the white hegemony of modernist art history. Moreover, their celebrity status has undermined the possibility of an oppositional discourse among the deprived and powerless that would expose African/Asian collusion with a system that refuses to come to terms with its colonial past and its legacies. No wonder that this success also coincided with the end of the 'Black Arts Movement' in Britain, which began its discourse in the avant-garde tradition of dissent and opposition.

The success of the system in maintaining its status quo was much strengthened with the fall of the Soviet bloc in the 1990s and the global triumph of neoliberal capitalism. The success and institutional celebration of some young artists from 'other' cultures today is an essential part of the success of the market economy at the global level in which all cultures are allowed to play their traditional roles. And with this has arisen the postcolonial Other – in various forms of ethnic, racial, cultural or political otherness – who is happy to be inside the system whatever it entails.

Nor is it any wonder that most artists today have succumbed to the pressures of globalised capital and the expansion of the art market and its constant appetite for exotic objects. My point is that most of the work of contemporary artists from the Third World, whether they live in the West or in their own countries, and particularly that work now being institutionally celebrated as part of the multiculturalism of the West, is not entirely what the artists might have produced had they been free to act historically by taking a radical position in art, or even as an expression of their imagination as free individuals. Those who pursue art as a profession and aspire to a successful career are subject to coercion by the power and benevolence of the West into producing something that does not pose any threat to the structures of Western institutions and their philosophical underpinning. The success of these artists can then also be used to create an illusion of change, to show that change does not mean abandoning old cultural forms, and that people can in fact benefit from staying within the boundaries of their own cultures.

With multiculturalism, and the success in the West of the present generation of artists from all over the world, the postcolonial struggle for equality seems to have come to an end; and with it the end of art as a critical discourse.

The issues I have raised here cannot be resolved by the expediency of multiculturalism or, to be more precise, by parading other cultures in the global arena. We cannot ignore the fact that most cultures do not have their own power of determination in this global scenario, as the ambition of the prevailing dominant system works against the basic needs and individual rights and freedom of a majority of people in the world. Individual freedom of expression, particularly when it comes to contemporary art practice, can neither be realised nor achieved when the means to express this freedom are predetermined by the dominant system on the basis of cultural specificity, even when this predetermination is supposedly for the benefit of many artists.

Chila Kumari Burman, (b Liverpool, England), *Into The Vortex Out In The World*, 2009, bindis, Indian and Thai stickers, fluorescent glitter, collage, gold leaf, fake gems, felp tip and inkjet on Somerset velvet, 30 x 22 inches

Cultural Diversity
and Institutional Policy

Jean Fisher

'Cultural diversity' has widely differing interpretations, from transparent initiatives to broaden inclusiveness to institutional policies that simply disguise political inequalities. However interpreted, the term almost always implies a majority monoculture against which all else is 'diverse', predicated on an hypostatisation of cultural and ethnic (or other) differences. Fundamentally, however, cultural diversity concerns social justice, because diversity debates surface in national contexts imprinted with legacies of injustice, inequality and discrimination against minority groups; and agency, defined as the freedom of individuals to act as political and creative subjects, within the limits of respect for the equal legitimate rights of others.

Any consideration of cultural diversity therefore cannot be thought outside universal human rights. This is already asserted in the United Nations Universal Declaration of Human Rights as an obligation upon the nation-state regardless of race, colour, sex, language, religion, political or other opinion, national or social origin, property, birth or other status,[1] and is based in the principle that such rights are morally non-negotiable and take precedence over geopolitical (ie national) interests. In recent years specific cultural rights have been elaborated by UNESCO's Universal Declaration on Cultural Diversity (UDCD) whose 'guidelines' emphasise that cultural diversity is an 'adaptive process' in which 'each individual must acknowledge not only otherness in all its forms but also the plurality of his or her own identity, within societies that are themselves plural'.[2] The cultural rights protected – subject to respect for human rights – include non-discriminatory freedom of creative expression and language, quality education, preservation of cultural heritage, and access to the means of expression and dissemination.

But certain problems present themselves: how can diverse, and sometimes antagonistic cultural perspectives and values be accommodated by *universal* human rights? How do governing states interpret the obligation and implement it in practice? The answer to these questions must begin with the understanding that culture is not a fixed object to be owned, but a continuously evolving way of life in which, in a democracy, conflictual interests are integral and therefore the notion that they can be 'resolved' is less convincing than accommodation through open dialogue. Throughout the latter half of the twentieth century it was the failure of central government to engage in dialogue with minority communities that turned disappointment into violent conflict. In multicultural, multi-faith societies, majority culture policies of assimilation or integration have too often been based on assumptions that a minority either has no culture, or would relinquish its cultural identity and adopt some idealised national monoculture; such policies do not account for either the contribution minority cultures make to national life, or the transformative, creative potential of intercultural exchanges. Significantly, Article 2 of the UDCD notes that policies of cultural *pluralism* – the inclusion and participation of all citizens – give 'expression to the reality of cultural diversity'. Hence, rather than institutional interpretations engineered to fit a narrowly defined monocultural perspective, one might look for policies that address basic values of humanity shared by all cultures: the hinge of universal human rights.

Given that over a period of thirty years British arts organisations under directives from central government have produced reports on 'cultural diversity', a fairly unique scenario presents itself from which to assess the context, nature and impact of diversity policies and initiatives on visual arts and artists.[3] A cursory glance at these reports suggests however that government policy initiatives have mostly been *reactive* responses to periods when 'minority' communities' despair at social injustice and disrespect boils over into visible social unrest; at which point short-term 'management' is sought, particularly through the cultural and educational spheres. That is, British government arts diversity initiatives have been intimately tied to what are, strictly speaking, *political* policies of social welfare and cohesion and, indeed, in a broader sense to concepts of social engineering.

Naseem Khan's initial, well-intentioned report, *The Arts Britain Ignores,* 1976, was a response to the exclusion of what Khan called 'ethnic minorities' from active engagement and decision-making in British cultural life, which is to say, the British national narrative. Cultural exclusion is a political issue insofar as it reveals the *limits* in the national status of minority constituencies as *fully constituted citizens,* a problem that has recently returned to haunt the British government vis-à-vis its Islamic constituencies. It highlights the fact that citizenship is not simply a legalistic or 'nationalistic' category, but entails reciprocal obligations on the part of government and the people to ensure both the sociopolitical security and the cultural wellbeing of all citizens.

From the perspective of visual arts, Khan's report set the terms for what was subsequently to be adopted by arts administrations as 'ethnic minority arts' (encompassing everything from the 'folkloric' to professional 'high' art) and which quickly became inseparable from the meaning of 'cultural diversity'. That these terms were accepted so uncritically by both sympathetic administrations and the majority of British African, African Caribbean and Asian artists is due largely to the fact that the mainstream art establishment was not a level playing field and 'positive discrimination' was seen as the only immediate answer to endemic institutional racism. This continues to be the case: in 2003 Arts Council England required that its RFOs (Regularly Funded Organisations) submit a 'Cultural Diversity Action Plan', with the implication that targets which included BME (Black Minority Ethnic) would be tied to funding. Nonetheless, whilst these reports have diagnosed institutional deficiencies, in many ways their recommendations and how they were implemented have been counter-productive, not least in the elusive sphere of artistic freedom.

Among the critical analyses of the history of British cultural diversity policies within the publicly funded visual arts sector is Richard Hylton's *The Nature of the Beast,* 2007.[4] Hylton points out a basic evaluative problem behind 'cultural diversity' agendas: 'The related notions that some people are more "culturally diverse" or more "ethnic" than others are equally problematic. "Ethnic minority" and "culturally diverse" are terms that privilege a limited notion of difference based on "race". Such notions are unhelpful, because they presuppose or imply normality to be white and everything else to be diverse.'[5] In addition, the historical 'apathy' and lack of proactive engagement of 'white' dominated arts institutions with cultural diversity reinforces the perception that, like racism, cultural diversity is seen to be the concern of 'ethnically diverse' people alone.

Two primary issues arise out of Hylton's analysis. Firstly, what are the implications in cultural diversity policies of categorising artists by racial or ethnic typologies? If artists' recognition and support is only based on such markers, it places the artist in a straightjacket of conformity that, on the one hand, risks crippling artistic creativity, and on the other, confines them to a limited range of 'thematic' shows and critical discourses. It also further marginalises those 'ethnic' artists who do not wish to be so categorised. To focus and judge work on the basis of ethnic or racial markers is, on the one hand, to look only for confirmation of expectation, even prejudice – the artist as anthropological 'native informer' – and on the other, to ignore the unique artistic dimension and experience of the work and to overlook its potential to deterritorialise monocultural assumptions of contemporary reality. It has been symptomatic of cultural diversity policies in general that a 'culturally different' artist is presumed to be 'representative' of that community (and during the 1980s the common policy was to employ 'ethnic' artists in community projects rather than the fine art field). Aside from this rarely being the case, given that most artists sustain pluralised and often agonistic cultural positions, this denies non-white artists the relative *aesthetic autonomy* that is understood by white artists to be their right, an autonomy that takes as its core the *idea of art* and art's entire history, not a narrow anthropological notion of culture. Nonetheless, despite Hylton's rather bleak analysis, over the past decade British 'ethnically diverse' artists have been able to distance themselves from these entrapments in terms of the *content* of their work, if not from the way they themselves are *positioned* in the art system.

Secondly, that institutional cultural diversity initiatives to increase the percentage of non-white participation in the art system – administrative, curatorial and artists' exhibitions – even if modestly successful (and Hylton claims that in fact there has been little improvement since the 1980s) have not fundamentally altered the *qualitative* structure of the system, or the attitudes that support it, so that existing power structures and relations remain intact.[6] Hylton notes that what emerges is a 'tick box' culture where lip service is paid to cultural diversity with periodic 'survey' shows of non-white artists, but no substantial increase in recognition of individuals.[7] Certainly, relatively few British 'minority' artists have gained private gallery support, or are selected to represent Britain in prestigious international shows, and most exhibition opportunities rely on publicly funded galleries and commissions. Hylton therefore recommends that policy directives, rather than target the 'excluded' should challenge 'those who do the excluding'. It is Hylton's contention that, insofar as cultural diversity policies continue to categorise individuals along racial or ethnic lines, and insofar as separate diversity funding provisions for 'black arts' absolve the more prestigious institutions and funders from engagement with 'minority' artists as independent practitioners alongside white artists, they have the effect of legitimising a *segregated* artworld.[8]

Among the modest shifts in British cultural diversity attitudes is the Mayor of London's policy document *Delivering Shared Heritage*, 2005, which draws on the expertise of a range of black and Asian cultural advisors.[9] While the commission was not specifically concerned with the visual arts, it is notable for attempting to reframe national heritage and its institutions as a shared patrimony of shared histories irrespective of 'racial' ancestries, although its focus remains on increasing the institutional and audience participation of African, African Caribbean and Asian constituencies (unlike the Khan report, which included Latin Americans and East Europeans amongst the 'ignored'). Of value here is the recognition that social and historical narratives are key to a sense of social cohesion and belonging. In fact, over the past two decades, the work of British black and Asian artists and film-makers, such as Zarina Bhimji, Black Audio Film Collective, Keith Piper, Isaac Julien and Shaheen Merali, has been instrumental in imaginatively plundering the 'forgotten' colonial archive to bring shared histories into the public domain. Re-narrating the past through the lens of the present towards a transformation of national narratives has been an important facet of artistic intervention in the broader social field.

Delivering Shared Heritage clearly takes its cue from UNESCO, citing Article 1 of the UDCD, and includes in its 'case for diversity' statutory imperatives, citizens' rights, national cohesion and identity, stimulating the knowledge economy, business, economic development and regeneration. While recognising that encouraging participation in arts and culture may be a more effective way of building an individual's sense of *citizenship* than more fraught and prescriptive notions of 'national identity' – which, as Benedict Anderson argued, is a largely 'imaginary' construction – like earlier reports, the underlying political philosophy of *Delivering Shared Heritage* bears further scrutiny.

The advocacy of 'sharing' is a positive move, but the concept of 'cultural heritage' does not escape the problem of how culture itself is defined. Cultural heritage is primarily understood as preserving the archive and those practices surviving from the past. As such, heritage claims, like those of cultural diversity, fall back on conservative anthropological definitions that see culture – and cultural identity – as a fixed set of terms, which again encourages segregation.[10] This leaves little space for conceiving culture (and identity) in the terms addressed by visual artists, namely, as a dynamic transformative process that is enriched by borrowings and exchanges across fuzzy borders. As already stated, culture is not a property to be owned but an experience lived, with all its attendant paradoxes and conflicts; as such it is a mistake to conflate culture with 'race' or 'ethnicity'.

The promotion of heritage as an 'agent for economic regeneration' betrays some complicity with a shift in government policies in which culture has become increasingly instrumentalised and subsumed within utilitarian, integrationist policies primarily addressing social cohesion, urban regeneration and economic viability. As Jonathan Vickery notes, within this emerging social instrumentalism, 'culture and creativity were means to generate an already existing process of social reconstruction, in which culture was conceived unquestioningly as wholly positive, not itself ridden by structural contradictions and conflicts, but which could create unproblematic modes of engagement with leisure, training, job creation and industry.'[11] The consequence, as he further notes, is that,

> under New Labour, the DCMS (Department of Culture, Media and Sport) and Arts Council, whatever their virtues, have not presented a credible policy challenge to the hegemony of social policy in the 'discourse' of urban regeneration, and that is in part due to a *weak concept of culture and an untheorised understanding of the relation between culture and society.* Consequently, cultural policy is either marginal, outside the mainstream of heavyweight urban and social policy areas, or is appended to these areas as a supplement.[12]

According to a 2002 DCMS document, the arts had to make a 'demonstrable contribution to Government social policy', notably in the areas of culture and community, a prescription with which Arts Council England subsequently complied, but which fosters national homogeneity rather than local particularity, and – insofar as they are subject to standardised performance indicators and the mantra of 'public accountability' – short-term, measurable goals focused on the popular end of the culture industry at the expense of long-term developments in 'quality of life' (another neo-humanist 'definition' of culture that New Labour has voiced but finds difficult to implement).

This is not to say that fine art practices do not contribute positively to social cohesion or urban regeneration, but as Vickery points out, none of the corporate policies described in recent Arts Council England documents concerns art as *such.* They concern art's socio-political function, confirming the Chair of Arts Council England's own admittance that there has been an unprecedented process of institutional isomorphism between Arts Council England and central government and loss of its prior, more independent, 'arm's length' status. [13] One may additionally ask how far this encroachment of political, economic and corporate 'interests' on the independence of arts specialists is paralleled by UNESCO's reconfiguration during the 1990s of an Executive Board no longer constituted by independent intellectuals and advisors but by delegates elected from or by members of Congress, and whether such shifts are a recipe for stifling the freedom and contribution to global debates of academic and artistic research. Any 'constitution of citizenship' has to take decisive steps beyond the concept of national sovereignty as it was elaborated throughout the history of nation-states. It must deepen and rearticulate the notion of 'popular sovereignty' in the sense of building an effective responsible international political leadership and direct representation of the population and its social interests, but in political terms – not 'ethnic' or 'cultural' ones – as against the current system of uncontrolled bureaucracy and hidden compromises among national politicians.

The predominance of justifications for the social value of culture, in which 'cultural diversity' is now an embedded factor, overlooks the crucial question of what culture – let alone fine art – is as a value and *end in itself.* As Vickery says, without a robust concept of culture it is not only difficult to formulate the relation between culture and society, but also the relation between culture and fine art (which, as Pierre Bourdieu described, has its own specialist infrastructure of language, rules and agents), and the place of professional visual artists – provided that one can still maintain the view that the visual arts are evolving practices relatively autonomous from ideological and political interference. Without an appropriate language, how is it possible to advance convincing political arguments for the integral role of artists and artistic autonomy in our global societies; or is artistic autonomy to be dismissed as an anachronism from an earlier, more elitist era? Institutional concepts of 'creativity' refer to broad education-orientated notions of developing individual 'expression', social identities and communications skills, but in practice do not necessarily involve fine artists; and where 'creativity' programmes exist with artists' involvement, development of the artist's own work is typically distinct from the programme. While 'creativity' programmes may provide the impulse for a young person's choice of art as a profession, they offer no insights into what 'creativity' means in the visual arts context. Public policy, as Vickery states, lacks a concept of culture 'that embodies both subject-specific values and socially-grounded action'.[14]

It is clear that the current condition of visual artists globally and the forms of artistic practices they employ cannot be separated from the complexities of the economic-political institutional contexts in which they function; and yet they are not reducible to them. Contemporary fine art practice is interdisciplinary in its research sources and understanding, and provides an intellectual value that cannot be trapped in market, political or social value systems. While governments may appropriate market-successful artists to their national agendas, this is not the sphere in which genuine artistic thought operates. Beyond institutional policies or directives, visual artists are themselves adept at imaginatively diagnosing, researching and expressing the complexities, aporias and systemic failures of our shared contemporary realities, often before political culture is aware of them. It is the failure of institutional policies that this rich vein of visionary thought is not drawn on at the *inception* of policy discussions but rather as a cosmetic afterthought.

Visual artists are also adept at traversing a plurality of social and cultural spaces, opening up new, non-market dependent networks of global exchange as well as sustaining older collaborative forms of artists' workshops and collectives, none of which, of course, can be effectively sustained without economic support. Over the past decades, most of the incisive critiques of contemporary reality under 'multiculturalism' and 'globalisation' have come from artists institutionally bracketed as 'culturally diverse'. They are 'national' artists, insofar as they respond to the specific historical conditions that a national society presents; but they are also 'transnational' insofar as their experience, alliances and insight extend beyond political borders, operating at the interface of multiple cultural identifications. In this sense they provide an overwhelmingly crucial role of *translation* – not only across disciplines and practices, but also across diverse cultural ideas and positions. It is from these artists that we learn to reconfigure the meaning of 'citizenship' as an inclusive, transnational cultural right, which means artists engaging *on their own terms* with the social sphere, negotiating between the aspirations of the local and the pressures of the global.

To a large extent political policies on cultural diversity suffer from similar problems to those that cripple debates on 'multiculturalism'. In both cases there is a difference between diversity and multiculturalism as lived experience and how they have been interpreted and implemented through political policies. In 1985 the Swann Report sensibly defined multiculturalism as promoting common values, respect for diversity, equality of opportunity, freedom of cultural expression and conscience, clearly in accordance with the principles of universal human and civil rights. Successive governments have, however, failed to implement these values by failing to address the sociopolitical roots of inequality and racism. Instead, policies have attempted to 'manage' diversity according to ethnicity: that is, homogenising individuals and communities into boxes that ignore both internal differences and external affiliations, giving in to conservative separatism (such as faith schools), and then policing the borders under the mantra of 'respecting difference'. As a consequence of these failings, all debates on multiculturalism have become discredited.

In sum, institutions have tended to regard cultural diversity as a policy exercise, implementing it through the occasional BME project, not through genuine structural reform. Reform cannot simply mean raising the percentage of BME actors in senior management and governing bodies; it must mean a radical review of core philosophy in which cultural pluralism is genuinely embedded throughout arts, education and heritage institutions. Culture and the visual arts have not been served by their subjection to the neoliberal capitalism of central government. The innovative benefits of cultural pluralism are often immeasurable and long-term, so do not have immediate 'economic' viability as marketable commodities: economics is the wrong yardstick by which to measure cultural efficacy or artistic intellectual value. The extent to which public arts funding has relinquished its responsibilities to the short-term interests of the private and corporate sector is a recipe for the stifling of art's autonomy and cultural innovation, where sustaining the richness of cultural diversity produced by 'ethnic minority' practitioners is likely to be a primary casualty in the long term unless more fluidity is encouraged between the public and private sectors under the current economic reality. Above all, cultural diversity initiatives should not be a substitute for failures in the political sphere, a point that our arts institutions should impress more forcefully on central government. What is needed are policies that work towards implementing a new British national narrative of cultural pluralism and tolerance based in universal human rights and aspirations that emphasise what we share and contribute as common humanity.

Towards an Inclusive British Community

Saleem Arif, (b 1949, Hyderabad), *On the Verge of Union with the Secret*, 1986–1987, oil on muslin and wood, 248 x 355 cm, collection: Mr and Mrs John and Ann Pare, London

Diversity after Diversity

Roshi Naidoo

INTRODUCTION

When I was commissioned to write this piece I was asked to pose some potential solutions to the problems associated with the ways in which the managerial discourses of diversity have played out in the arts and heritage sector, rather than just revisit familiar critiques of the agenda. After all, the critical arguments have had numerous airings in public forums, policy documents and academic writing. Why are issues of diversity always loaded at the service delivery end of an arts organisation's priorities – always to do with 'new' audiences, education and young people – and not integrated into the bedrock of every aspect of its work? Why are the people employed to 'do diversity' often treated like piece workers and brought in only for one-off, temporary, online exhibitions, or education projects for Black History Month? Why does expertise in, for example, the Black Arts movement in 1980s Britain, not translate into an appreciation that such expertise does not preclude other knowledge or competencies, and that it may be an asset, rather than a barrier, to becoming a leader of a mainstream arts organisation? How has the ghost of 1970s multiculturalism and the dreaded 'saris, samosas and steel bands' ideology returned in various guises to haunt discussions of how best to represent black and Asian arts in Britain, and also found new tokenistic expression around other issues of difference?

I could go on. But if we are moving forward, should we be rehashing these critiques or not? Perhaps we should be looking at the enormous strides forward that have been made through institutional diversity initiatives, such as noting the list of senior personnel from the sector who have been engaged with the Greater London Authority's Heritage Diversity Task Force (HDTF).

The important thing I think is not to present either a hagiography or a rubbishing of the diversity agenda (and no, I am not suggesting a 'third way'). The issue is not about being 'for' or 'against' diversity policy as it stands, but about something more nuanced, which challenges the limitations of the ideological, philosophical and historical lens through which we view the very idea of what diversity means.

It is for that reason that we need to explore existing criticisms before we can shift towards more progressive formations.

This article then will look at the theoretical and political assumptions that underlie current policy, as well as examining those that underpin suggested changes to that agenda, before I move on to potential ways forward. As we know, we need to do some major rethinking to find solutions to the shortcomings of the policy, process and practices of diversity, rather than just make cosmetic changes around recruitment quotas. But despite a widespread acceptance of this (at a national level at least), discourses of 'diversity' stop short of asking some of the more difficult questions. And that may be because substantive rethinking involves words and phrases that have become unfashionable in the sector recently, such as politics, power and structural inequality.

LISTENING TO HUSHED CONVERSATIONS

I began by noting that critiques of the diversity agenda have had a good airing in various forums. In some ways this is true, but in others it is not. Where they do not get a good airing is in the day-to-day work of arts and heritage organisations, where the best and most illuminating criticisms of diversity can be heard in hushed discussions muttered in quiet corners. Such conversations are whispered because the weight of the discourse of diversity, and the unrelenting and often disproportionate enthusiasm with which each 'inclusive' project is met, can hang over formal meetings and discussions about difference and representation in oppressive ways, making people unable to speak. It is through listening to the informal conversations of sector workers who are both struggling to have issues of sexuality, disability, 'race' and difference mainstreamed in the arts, and/or are themselves 'different' in some way, and simply wishing to pursue a career in the sector without being straitjacketed into being a representative of one aspect of their identity, that we can find keys and clues as to how to move forward.

For example, when, in my capacity as an arts and heritage consultant, I am shown images of the latest youth project featuring prominent pictures of young Asians in hijabs, sponsored by some multinational company and told that the organisation is 'very excited', how do I say that this does not excite me? How churlish does it sound to be unenthusiastic about young people being empowered to speak in a public forum about identity and belonging through the medium of the arts? But it really does not excite me and these are some of the reasons why.

Firstly, for those of us who have been around for a while, this focus on youth is something very familiar. We believed once that this was a precursor to a more embedded approach, but the attention given to the young in diversity projects around 'race' seems not to be replicated so enthusiastically beyond this age group. (Interestingly there seems to be much less interest in young people and issues of sexuality.) This has the effect of constantly reinventing a non-white presence in Britain as new and the future, rather than a long-standing historical fact. Therefore diversity and representation are always positioned as either being in a state of embryonic development or a 'work in progress' for institutions. Those who challenge the sector's sluggishness then are simply carping and need to be more patient. The unspoken attitude of many who spearhead diversity projects is this: look at all the great work we are doing with young Muslims in a deprived area of London – it will only be matter of time till this seeps through right across the organisation.

I am not arguing that arts projects with these young 'diverse' people cannot be valuable, important or illuminating, but they need to be part of a wider politics of representation and empowerment. Otherwise the same young people who may find inspiration working with an arts organisation now, and as a result are encouraged to pursue a career in the sector, may well find themselves in a ghetto ten years down the line, only talking about the 'experiences' of migrant communities, or fronting projects about changes in British identity, rather than having access to the same opportunities as their peers from the 'right' backgrounds.

When the word 'diversity' is heard, particularly in local and regional arts sectors, and not followed immediately by 'youth' or 'new audiences', another term one can perhaps hear is 'Caribbean elders'. This is one of the instances where listening to informal conversations is very illuminating. A colleague once told me this homogenising of 'elders' annoyed her, but felt she could not really say in meetings that this term was not only sentimentalising and disempowering, but also vaguely racist. Another person told me that there was a time when you could find references to the same group of Caribbean 'elders' mentioned as consultants in a raft of funding applications and diversity projects, and that this was a worry which was hard to voice, especially when the group in question were understandably flattered at being regularly courted.

What the two points about 'youth' and 'elders' illustrate is the lack of space to properly interrogate the complex political assumptions that underpin diversity as a managerial discourse. It is extremely difficult for individuals in meetings to raise these concerns without appearing to be horrible people who do not care about giving expression to the old, the young or other socially excluded groups, such as refugees. National institutions may in general be more nuanced in how they approach diversity, but the absence of day-to-day opportunities to question the back story, if you like, means that the perpetual 'excitement' expressed creates a momentum which is hard to counter. After all, who wants to prevent the tangible action of a youth diversity project by bogging people down in theory?

The second reason why I cannot share in such enthusiasm relates to the politics of identity. Increasingly institutions create the conditions whereby people are defined too rigidly through singular aspects of their identity. The arts and heritage sector does not simply reflect identities 'out there' when they organise people into categories such as 'young Muslims' through diversity initiative. They also create them. Political, cultural, social and 'ethnic' identities are not fixed, hermetically sealed groupings that simply require representation in public sector organisations. The process of identity negotiation and renegotiation is a complex one and requires a sophisticated understanding of notions of difference, representation and power. Institutions may be offering a voice to individuals or communities who have been neglected, but that offer may be highly contingent on a foregrounding of one aspect of their identity at the expense of others.

People inhabit a multitude of identities without them being necessarily in conflict with each other, and it is through art, film, music and literature that those identities – overlapping, competing, fluid and inspiring – are expressed. It is through the arts that one can find narratives that challenge reductive assumptions about what 'other' people are 'like', or what everyday life looks like in different parts of the world. Yet too often diversity policy in the sector takes a narrow instrumentalist view and misses the opportunity to reflect on the multiple meanings of identity in their quest for easily delineable categories of subjects. What is lost in this process? How are people reduced and diminished as well as empowered? Once again, this is a difficult concern to articulate.

We also require some space to discuss why it is in the sector's interest to pursue current formations of reflecting diversity. Demonstrating that they are relevant across all communities helps legitimise the authority of our public institutions. But are they up front about this, or does it feel as though they are being inclusive as an act of magnanimity? We also have to ask questions regarding a potential correlation between projects that reflect the voices and concerns of Muslim communities at the same time that we as a nation are engaged in a 'war on terror'. As the morality of current conflicts are played out in political debate, a bizarre boundary between 'good and 'bad' Muslims is being created in the popular imagination. The arts and heritage sector needs to play a sharper role in challenging these limiting ways of understanding people as individuals, communities and citizens. As economist and political theorist Amartya Sen notes in his book *Identity and Violence:*

> Indeed, the increasingly common use of religious identities as the leading – or sole – principle of classification of the people of the world has led to much grossness of social analysis. There has been, in particular, a major loss of understanding in the failure to distinguish between 1) the various affiliations and loyalties a person who happens to be Muslim has, and 2) his or her Islamic identity in particular.[1]

And it is also to this end that the sector needs to challenge the issue that constitutes my third reason for failing to be excited. The slippage between 'diversity' and 'faith' as terms has steadily increased. This has now been going on for so long that for some they are perceived as the same thing. It is again one of those things very difficult to raise objections to, especially as we live in a time when the right and far-right are clearly underpinned by Islamophobia. These groups attempt to legitimate their reactionary, unpleasant and illogical views by playing on reductive notions of 'Islam', and liberal institutions have played an important role in challenging this. However, the same institutions can also lock people into oppressive binaries through this process, and should instead attempt to formulate a more nuanced approach to issues of faith and secularity. And part of this is developing a politics of diversity that is distinct from faith, and not applied in a lazy fashion to every aspect of difference.

This need for distinction is constantly felt. For example, at an event at a major museum recently a curator talked about a project whereby representatives from faith groups came in to change object labels and situate them within a more pertinent religious context. When I raised questions about the multitude of problems this might pose –given that even within each faith grouping the meaning of an object can change dramatically – I was dismissed. In the ladies toilet, though, someone approached me and said that I had raised an important point, but felt they could not say so for fear of being labelled as culturally insensitive. Most senior staff in the sector will acknowledge that this is a hugely problematic area, and they do understand that fighting racism and criticising religion are not incompatible positions. But without a mechanism through which to express this, things become difficult and it is easier to say nothing. Secularity in public culture is not a given but something that has been fought for over centuries, and is never so secure that it does not require protecting. It would be a shame if the unravelling of the first threads were performed because of diversity policies, especially when, once again, the arts and heritage sector is so perfectly positioned to make interesting, subtle and politically crucial points about identity, community and belonging available to a wider public.

And so to the fourth reason that I so often find myself cringing, rather than jumping for joy, at diversity project meetings. This relates to something I have referred to elsewhere as a fear of sameness.[2] I have made the point that a fear of 'sameness' can be detected in diversity policies, and that while there is space to accommodate the superficial differences of 'minorities' in public culture, it is in acknowledging the 'sameness' of 'minorities' – as well as a fear of difference – that prevents us having our full humanity represented in public sector institutions, the media, academia and elsewhere. For example, understanding that British history cannot be separated from colonial history does not make someone a 'diversity' person. Furthermore, this understanding and, say, an expertise in the Harlem Renaissance, does not preclude other expertise. As I have pointed out,

> some of us do actually also know about European art and Hollywood film and the history of punk rock etc. But we become fragmented within the sector – our racial identities either overdetermined or dangerously ignored.[3]

The creeping worry is that too many people seem to believe that there is one big topic called 'diversity', and that it is easier as an arts organisation to fulfil a remit for it by engaging with people who are different in the 'right' way – preferably visibly. Again it is worth listening to what people say in the canteen, and I have heard over and over again the view that around 'race', institutions are more comfortable with people who can more easily be designated as 'foreign', rather than with 'other' Europeans with a deep and complex history of being embedded in the continent over many generations, and possessing a set of cultural competencies and interests which sit uncomfortably within the diversity agenda.

To reiterate, we need sober analysis to replace all this 'excitement' about diversity. It strikes me that to be excited by it as it stands is like being excited by a university prospectus which fronts images of black students in the mistaken belief that the philosophical or literary canon on its courses represents a sea change in how colonialism and Empire are taught.

I have provided broad brush strokes here and not included the many projects, exhibitions, art installations and so on that *do* challenge limited definitions of what 'diversity' means. However, I think that the characterisations I have sketched above do hold water, especially if one looks beyond the handful of enlightened movers and shakers in the sector who wish to improve how the arts responds to the questions of difference and representation. So while all this might sound 'negative' and appear not to propose ways forward, I think that it is an important exercise. And for this reason we need to analyse not only institutional diversity policy, but also the different criticisms of it before we can proceed to solutions.

CRITIQUING THE CRITICS

There are no shortages of criticism for diversity, both as an actual policy and as an imagined and manufactured threat to 'our' culture and heritage. These come framed within a range of ideologies, and even when they appear similar on the surface, they are motored by different political interests. In discussing a fear of sameness, I have been careful to distinguish this from the liberal notion that we are all 'just people' and therefore should not be bothered with all this difference nonsense.[4] This usually works as a strategy to deny the validity of differing subject positions and to downplay the impact of homophobia, racism, class prejudice and other forms of intolerance on people's everyday lives.

Therefore I can be suspicious of arguments that suggest that if it were not for the relentless focus on difference through diversity policies in the cultural sector, artists could be just artists and judged on merit alone. The report 'Boxed In', produced by the Manifesto Club Artistic Autonomy Hub, airs this view, albeit more cogently and subtly.5 The report, authored by Sonya Dyer, attacks the Arts Council's specific policies for increasing the participation of black and 'ethnic minority' people in the sector as artists, curators and leaders, and concludes that initiatives such as the Arts Council's decibel and Inspire programmes segment people through the crude racial categorisation of their work and abilities. In the case of artists, this denies them their uniqueness of being simply artists, and is counterproductive to the development of their careers. It not only leads to a culture of paternalism and dependency, but also to a reductive view of the arts as a conduit through which to improve society in relation to equalities. This does chime with the concerns over 'diversity' expressed by a range of other critics. However, as I have noted, it is important to distinguish between different critiques of the equalities agenda and to locate arguments within their wider contexts.

'Manifesto', the group that produced 'Boxed In', is committed to libertarian 'freedoms', and is reflective of a strand of thought coming from the right and libertarian groups within which an indictment of New Labour's cultural policy leads to a general attack on 'multiculturalism' and what is termed the 'race relations industry'. On their web pages one can also find their 'freedom of flight' campaign and a castigation of Heathrow protesters who 'caused delays for families'. The freedom not to die in an environmental catastrophe is not discussed. I do not mention this to be glib, but because we must follow the trajectory of where such politics takes us. 'Boxed In' is a very clear and thoughtful reflection on some of the problems of diversity initiatives. But we have to look closely at the details and ask ourselves if we are being led to old reactionary positions, albeit in new, trendier clothes. What solutions are being proposed? Are we being asked to return to the notion of individuals on a level playing field with no need for the political interference of the state – a merging of the liberal humanism of our sameness with the belief that all are equal under the market? Diversity policies may indeed smack of paternalism, but how much more paternalistic would a future anti-state agenda be, on the basis of the idea that social problems are best 'solved' by philanthropists?

Criticisms of diversity can be part of a wider agenda to undermine the public sector and give freer reign to the private – no doubt so the private sector can make as good a job of governing the arts as it has of the banks.

Therefore, although we should take very seriously all critiques of diversity policies, we need to be aware of the political impetus behind some arguments for change. One particular remark in 'Boxed In' jumped out at me. Dyer notes: 'There is an equal lazy equation of "blackness" with "disability"... as if blackness were a disability in itself.'[6] Though I understand the broader point about institutions lumping all 'others' together, it is also a political understanding that disability and 'race' do have much in common. Disability politics have helped us to understand the ways in which people are made unable to participate in the public sphere, and made invisible in heritage culture, in ways not related to their impairment.[7] The troubling element in this quote is not just its lack of solidarity, but also the refusal to understand and challenge structural inequalities in favour of a singular focus on the rights of individual artists. For many libertarians and new conservatives, diversity politics is simply another interference in our lives, like too many road safety signs.

Balancing the politics of identity and difference with the politics of our common humanity has historically been a difficult philosophical problem. But we must understand how this has developed and understand the dialectic of identity politics. Civic culture has grown out of these contestations around difference – not in spite of them. And these interventions have been most successful when articulated through an understanding of power relations and structural inequalities. Criticising cultural diversity policy from a position which implies that doing away with it puts us all on a level playing field is not helpful unless it faces the thorny question of how to challenge homophobia, economic inequality, disablism, racism, sexism, etc.

SOLUTIONS

So you may say that it is easy for someone like me working as a consultant, and not within the strictures of one institution, to make criticisms, but what can people inside actually do? Most importantly they can embark on a more considered analysis of diversity policy as it exists, and can ask questions about what can change. This will require work, reading, thinking and considered consultation. An interest in bharatanatyam dancing, for example, is not in itself a qualification for someone to do an organisation's diversity work. There needs to be a more profound theoretical engagement with the field. Below is a rudimentary list of suggestions:

1   Move from thinking about 'inclusion' to a paradigm of 'cultural democracy'. The paternalistic notions associated with the former prevent sector staff from understanding that we all have cultural rights, and it is those which should be met, rather than an organisation's need to prove their commitment to diversity through tick-box exercises. As James Early from the Smithsonian Institute has said: 'You cannot invite me into my house – I am a citizen'.[8]

2   Stop 'celebrating' us. The fact that we live in a 'diverse' society is not a cause for 'celebration', but a simple and banal fact. We cannot seem to displace a central 'normal' figure in the middle of this against whom 'diversity' is measured. For example, for whom is 'multiculturalism' vibrant, exciting and new? Perhaps it is time to stop banging on about adding colour to the capital, or making the 2012 Olympic bid look attractive, and just accept it as a everyday fact of life, an historical legacy of colonialism, part of the intercultural dynamism and exchange that characterises all cultures and civilisations, and also an effect of contemporary global flows of capital and labour. It is not that I object to festivals that celebrate historically quashed identities, but difference needs to be acknowledged outside of, as well as through, Carnival, Chinese New Year, Pride, and the ubiquitous local multicultural festivals. And to paraphrase Ziauddin Sardar, rather than to be celebrated, we need power, and that comes from occupying the mainstream.[9]

3   Open up the possibilities of identity. By resisting the temptation to lock people into singular aspects of their identity, we can move to a place where people are allowed to be different, and the same, in many ways. Only through mainstreaming all these discussions can we see the full range of possibilities there are to enrich cultural expression and understanding through this. For example, accepting that a British Asian may find the band *The Smiths* more interesting than the fusion music of say, Nitin Sawhney, opens up all sorts of landscapes for cultural analysis. Such an interest is not 'white', and also may or may not involve reconciling a love of music which, to paraphrase, 'says something to them about their life', with the shifting racial politics of the author of these sentiments. But where we are at the moment means that only one of these artists is associated with 'diversity'. Everyone who is 'other' in some way will have a dozen similar examples of the limits of diversity as a discourse to accommodate and reflect the many different ways in which they experience and express their cultural identities. We really need properly to unleash the power of the arts to make sense of all this.

4   The arts and heritage sector needs to think about how diversity policy can make a real impact on challenging racism, sexism, homophobia, disablism, class and economic inequality. It also needs to think about the relationship between how it frames this, and broader issues of global justice, democracy and representation, whether that relates to understanding asylum or what constitutes British national culture. Rather than dwelling any more on politically toothless forms of diversity, policies should be reformulated to think about structural inequalities and cultural democracy. For example, is there a connection between the almost total ignorance in this country of the economic relationships between Britain and its former colo-

nies, and forms of popular racism and anti-immigration feeling? Those who set the cultural diversity agenda for museums, galleries, archives and the arts, would do well to focus on how their work impacts on such attitudes to 'race' and migration in Britain, rather than continuing their obsessive focus on one-off projects for black and Asian youth.

5 Go for the long-term over the short term. Stop focusing solely on the money your arts organisation has been awarded for a diversity project and the short time scale you have to deliver tangible outcomes. Think instead about the deeper, long-term institutional shifts that have to occur to place a concept of diversity at the centre of all work. And then ask yourself whether the concept of diversity you are working with is good enough. Is it engaged with equality and democracy or is it patronising, limiting and self-aggrandising?

CONCLUSION

Maybe this moment of reassessment should be grasped as an opportunity to give diversity narratives a stronger critical and progressive dimension. And for those who believe that it should not be political, we should remember that it already is, and that diversity is sold as a marketable commodity. Perhaps too we should use this moment to challenge the flat universe that is emerging in the sector, whereby too many things are deemed 'exciting' and innovative, and where space for critical voices can be limited. We know that if diversity is to be integrated into every aspect of the Art's Council's work it must be reformulated. But to do that we do need some 'back to the drawing board' thinking, and the freedom to question and criticise in public, without being positioned as negative.

In the end, this should not be simply about recruiting a better range of curatorial or managerial staff. It is should not just be about establishing permanent exhibitions that mainstream 'diverse' arts. Both these things are important, but something more profound has to happen. What is required is a philosophical and attitudinal change in how we perceive our national culture. It is about ridding people of the erroneous view that 'diversity' is only of interest to those who possess some form of 'otherness'. It is about a willingness to be open to the limitless cultural landscapes that have yet to be explored beyond the suffocating categories of identity we imprison people in. But if we do seize this opportunity, the power of the arts to transform will become palpable.

Cultural Inequality, Multicultural Nationalism and Global Diversity
Tate Encounters: Britishness and Visual Culture

Andrew Dewdney, David Dibosa and Victoria Walsh

When you go through the door... [to 'ambivalent mainstreaming'] it is a dangerous territory, it is an incredibly tricky territory and all sorts of monsters are waiting on the other side to assimilate you up.

Stuart Hall (2006)[1]

Is the era and the goal of 'cultural diversity' in the arts now over? Has the globalisation of the art world – 'let a thousand biennales bloom' – 'solved' the problem?

Stuart Hall (2010)[2]

INTRODUCTION

For some time now Britain has been experiencing a crisis in liberal/left progressive thinking about cultural diversity, which has opened the cultural field to an emergent and aggressive critique of 'cultural welfarism' and its instrumentalist policies. In the place of New Labour cultural policies, these new positions seek to maintain the legitimacy of cultural value based upon a nationalist and Eurocentric model of arts heritage coupled with cultural entrepreneurship. There is nothing startlingly new in this remix of heritage and enterprise and it is not the first time that this conservative emphasis has been the basis of arts policy. As this emphasis unfolds in future government policies it will be a matter of traditional emphasis and choice. However, in an equal and apparently opposite response to the increasingly common recognition of the problems of cultural instrumentalism within the professional cultural sector, the left/liberal position has been to extend the underlying entitlement argument of cultural welfarism to that of social justice as a means of promoting cultural equality. In what is a difficult argument to make, because it appears divisive, it can be argued that this extension to the idea of the museum of social justice conceptually continues the discourse of social exclusion and cultural deficit. Centrally, it continues with a practical programme of access, education and multiple voice perspectives that reproduces the very boundaries between mainstream and margins it seeks to dissolve.

Both the New Labour and New Conservative positions on culture accept a political gradualism which seems not to recognise the pace of global change. The argument here is that in cultural policy terms the political differences in positions which have been identified are in effect two sides of the same coin of British multiculturalism which is failing to grasp the new conditions and forces of capital and labour now propelling people, products and profits hither and thither across the globe.

A recent conference, 'From the Margins to the Core? An international conference exploring the shifting roles and increasing significance of diversity and equality in contemporary museum and heritage policy and practice', held at the Victoria and Albert Museum, London, in conjunction with the School of Museum Studies at the University of Leicester (2010) was one such attempt to review the progress of multiculturalism within the museum sector.[3] The conference assembled a formidable set of contributors from the British museum and galleries sector to address questions of embedding diversity, widening participation and establishing social justice in both museum policy and programmes. Tate Encounters, a three-year collaborative research project, contributed to the conference on the basis of an analysis of its fieldwork in which two major assertions were made. First, that enabling and inclusion practices of the museum, based upon unexamined social demographic categories set by government funding, could only shore up distinctions between a margin and the core and, in the case of BME (Black and Minority Ethnic) categories, could only reproduce a racialised view of human subjects. Second, it was argued that far from cultural diversity policy representing a central challenge to the core values of the museum, the implementation practices aimed at increasing equality and diversity were used to contain and manage the risk of external challenge to the core. These are the bold outlines of an argument that in detail needs much more space to evidence. However, the point here is that some amongst the conference organisers and participants disputed such a position, seeing it as a mischaracterisation of the efforts of work around diversity policy development that had taken place historically, identifying it, interestingly in what follows, as a neo-conservative position. This article explores in more detail the arguments contained in this response in an attempt to understand the limits of multicultural debate and where it might usefully be opened out and taken in the future.

TRICKY TERRITORIES

In 2006 London South Bank University (LSBU) was awarded a major research grant from the Arts and Humanities Research Council (AHRC) strategic research programme, Diasporas, Migration and Identities. The grant was to fund a three-year study in collaboration with Tate Britain and Wimbledon College of Art to consider the obstacles to access for diasporic communities to the national collection of British art held at Tate Britain. The project was titled 'Tate Encounters: Britishness and Visual Culture'.[4] The emergence of the AHRC national research funding stream coincided with an additional research initiative launched by the national Economic and Social Research Council (ESRC), Identities and Social Action Programme. In part, both of these initiatives can be located in the context and aftermath of the political and academic debates sparked by the Macpherson Report into the Metropolitan Police's handling of the murder of Stephen Lawrence. The report was singular in pointing to institutional racism in terms of 'The collective failure of an organisation to provide an appropriate and professional service to people because of their colour, culture, or ethnic origin.'[5]

In 2000 the Runnymede Trust published the Parekh Report on the future of multi-ethnic Britain. In commenting upon the institutions of the arts, media and sports the report stated:

> But the overall message of the chapter, in the words of a specialist who gave evidence to the Commission, is that 'the arts and media sectors do not see any implications for themselves in the Macpherson Report', for they do not recognise that institutional racism needs urgently to be addressed within their own domains.[6]

In prefacing its recommendations the report insisted that

> The concepts of equality and diversity must be driven through the government machinery at national and regional levels. Responsibility for making them real must be devolved to the local levels at which theory becomes practice, where real change does or does not take place. Verbal and financial commitment from the government is essential, but the test of real change is what happens on the ground.[7]

The Parekh Report reflected the evident desire for real change, highlighting the need for coherent policy, audits of existing practice, target setting and financial penalties, all similar to the practical approach of the Macpherson Report. A decade further on and we might now consider how much progress has been made in embedding the concepts of equality and difference in our national cultural institutions.

In the forging of the research collaboration between LSBU, Tate Britain and Wimbledon College of Art that formed Tate Encounters lay three mutual understandings: first, that despite over a decade of substantial dedicated funding and activity framed by policies of 'cultural diversity' that no significant increase in art museum attendance had been realised in 'minority' audiences; second, that academic debates centred around postcolonialism had not notably entered into curatorial discourse or practice; and third, that museological debates had not opened up a space in the art museum where policy and practice might meaningfully engage with each other to form a new model of curatorship – or indeed audience engagement.

At the heart of Tate Encounters lay the ambition to interrogate and analyse the connections and disconnections between the policies and theories of cultural diversity and their playing out in practice. This move into and through the art museum could be seen to represent one of Stuart Hall's 'tricky moments' for all members of the research team. In creating the conditions for the emergence of a reflexive enquiry, the project's endeavour was marked by a desire not to reproduce accounts of power and dominion over knowledge and representation in the art museum, but to arrive at a working account of the key issues that have both defined and confined the project of 'cultural diversity' work in a national cultural institution. Arriving at a new description of how cultural diversity operated at Tate Britain involved a constant negotiation with the institutional discursive location that a research project so obviously focused upon cultural diversity occupied in relationship to its perceived context of multiculturalism.

The politics of multiculturalism do not form part of the historical or naturalised context of the art museum but are inherently entwined in the contractual obligations to central government, primarily through the Department of Culture, Media and Sport's 'Public Sector Agreements' with national institutions such as Tate. Following on from a plethora of action reports produced by the Arts Council of England during the late 1990s and early 2000s, the National Museum Directors' Conference (NMDC) formed a Cultural Diversity Working Group in 2004, which concluded in 2006 'the need for a step change' in addressing issues of access and representation.[8] On each side of Hall's door of ambivalent mainstreaming, in and outside of institutions, opinions on the best ways to promote equality and the recognition of difference were complex and contested. The publication in 2006 of Munira Mirza's *Culture Vultures: Is UK Arts Policy Damaging the Arts?*[9] and Sonya Dyer's 2007 report *Boxed In* made evident a moment of the challenge and dissent in these debates and was notably followed by Richard Hylton's vociferous attack in *The Nature of the Beast* (2007) in which he declared,

> Since the 1970s, cultural diversity initiatives within the visual arts sector
> have arguably exacerbated, rather than confronted, exclusionary pathologies
> of the art world. They have compounded the problems of tokenism and racial
> separation within the arts sector.[10]

Stuart Hall's warning of 'ambivalent mainstreaming', sounded at an event at Tate Britain in 2006, came as the final building stages of the new home for INIVA were being completed at Rivington Place. During this panel discussion, initiated by Mike Phillips as Curator: Cross-Cultural Programmes at Tate Britain, Hall made a recurring plea to retrieve and to sustain the historical specificity of the conditions and contexts in which the proposition of cultural diversity had emerged and entered into common currency 'like sliced bread'. Hall saw clearly that the loss of collective historical memory had divested multiculturalism of its value and that any collapse of different generational relations and motives in the quest of migrant artists to join the project of modernity would end in the diversion of another moment of assimilation. In contrast, Hall and others recognised postwar commonwealth migration and the generations which came after as a longer process of globalisation which had been identified and announced eleven years previously during INIVA's seminal conference at Tate Britain on 'The New Internationalism'.

In the contemporary visual arts, the history and current identity crisis of INIVA is a good example of the unforeseen consequences of the conflicting discourses of multiculturalism and cultural diversity in relation to the continuing processes of globalisation. The tensions and contradictions of this expanded field of modernism, anticipated by the INIVA conference, but now framed by a new turn to internationalism through emerging new non-Western markets, revealed itself quite clearly in the research of Tate Encounters in two specific ways. First, throughout the two-year fieldwork period, self-selected students from LSBU who came from diasporic backgrounds readily identified in Tate Britain a call to their attention as the subjects of cultural diversity policy, while simultaneously experiencing Tate Modern as subjects of a global unregulated culture. Second, during one of over forty public discussions carried out as part of the Tate Encounters: Research in Process, artists including Hew Locke, Raimi Gbadamosi and Faisal Abdu'Allah readily noted how they felt implicitly framed by policies of cultural diversity and Britishness at Tate Britain, while at Tate Modern they assumed the status of 'international' artists. This conflation of identity with the local politics of cultural diversity at Tate Britain contrasted with the perception of artistic autonomy and subjectivity at Tate Modern offers a clue to the extent to which the racialisation of cultural diversity policy has obfuscated and indeed delimited the invitation not only to a diversity of artists but to audiences as well.[11]

At an early stage of Tate Encounters, we came to see in stark terms that defining the barriers to cultural access or entitlement in terms of those not represented in the museum, either as artists, professionals or visitors, was framed and overwritten by the discourse of social exclusion, which, without recourse to an understanding of the museum's present inclusions, practices and reproductions, positioned all of those outside of the museum as implicitly lacking some cultural value. Importantly, Tate Encounters was made to see by its voluntary participants that invitations to the museum based upon racialised or ethnicised identities reproduced a structural inequality from the outset, and whilst such inclusive overtures were aimed at redressing some unspoken cultural deficit, left the culture of the museum without challenge.

The Tate Encounters research continues to point to a new set of cultural conditions in which the imagined 'excluded subject' of widening participation perfectly understands the offer of the museum, but cannot meaningfully accept the museum's terms of engagement, whilst the museum, for its part, struggles to understand the new authority of this subject and hence is unable to recognise, or produce, a new audience. The research points to cultural developments in which the transcultural experience of migration, based upon global capital and labour flow, together with the transmedial experience of digital culture, now places every individual museum professional in exactly the same cultural space as that of every other individual subject in respect of the meaning of museum objects. If this is broadly correct, it denotes far-reaching implications for the project's view of cultural policy, education and the role of museums.[12]

In parallel with the studies of 'excluded subjects', Tate Encounters also developed an evidence base for accounting for the ways in which cultural diversity policies have circulated within institutional networks and for what work they do. The research developed an analysis that suggests that cultural diversity operates institutionally as the management of risk to the longer term, and some would argue central purposes of the museum, which are those of acquisition, collection and conservation. On this view cultural diversity networks are far from open, or rhizomatic, but function as institutional enclaves and narrow channels of communication cut off from larger networks of both private and public extension.[13]

More broadly the project has come to understand many of the responses to the Tate Encounters analysis to date as a significant apprehension, if not reluctance, on the part of practitioners to abandon the politics of identity and representation as the historic basis for progressive cultural engagement. This, it is argued, is a sign of a larger intellectual and political problem that is articulated as the limits of multiculturalism.

DISCERNING THE FAULT LINES
In March 2009 Tate Encounters ran a four-week series of public discussions at Tate Britain as part of its 'Research in Process' methodology. There were four strands to the discussions which involved contributions from artists, academics and practitioners contributing to the attempt to articulate a cultural and political his-

tory of the British art museum's response to cultural difference.[14] One event, 'The Changing Status of Difference: Cultural Policy from 1970 to the Present', serves well in discerning the lines along which the crisis discussed above continues to be shaped.[15] The three panelists spanned a period of arts policy development from the early 1980s to the present, encompassing practices and perspectives within the Arts Council, the Greater London Council, the NMDC and the Greater London Authority. The panel consisted of Baroness Lola Young of Hornsey, Munira Mirza, Director of Policy, Arts, Culture and the Creative Industries, Greater London Authority, and Sandy Nairne, Director, National Portrait Gallery.

Lola Young voiced a number of narrative threads across her own participation and involvement in the practical politics of diversity over this period, identifying the shifting language in which issues of diversity had been negotiated and how cultural policy initiatives, however well intentioned, inevitably reproduced a positioning of the subject as 'other'. For Young, the very term 'cultural diversity' was just the latest cipher for 'other' in a binary logic which out of frustration had led her to engage with the politics of representation intellectually defined by Stuart Hall and Paul Gilroy. She further marked herself as someone who had argued, and continues to argue, from the position of a cultural practitioner, academic and politician for a complex politics of cultural representation. From the perspective of the Tate Encounters' research Lola Young's recognition of the binary logic of racialised thinking is well made and parallels the logic of Tate Encounter's fieldwork. In addition, her call for a more complex cultural politics of representation, one that goes beyond the simple multicultural populist model of a fair aggregate of cultural bits, as well as a policy that is not based upon a market view of culture, is also germane to the current debate.

Sandy Nairne addressed directly the politicisation of culture and recognised how interior and narrowly focused the discussion of art and society had been during his time at both Tate and the Arts Council, as well as more generally within British contemporary visual arts in the 1970s. He saw that the setting of targets for proportional funding for BME arts at the Arts Council in the 1980s was no more than tokenism and went on to identify his own and others' recognition of the need for 'structural change' in who controlled cultural programming. At the Arts Council this had led to a raft of initiatives aimed at promoting ethnic minority arts, including decibel, INIVA and the building of Rivington Place. Finally, in his time as Director of the National Portrait Gallery he acknowledged that since the National Museum Directors' Conference working party in 2004 on staffing and governance, little had changed and that the then Minister for the Arts and Culture, David Lammy, had essentially told the Directors' group that it was not for the government to lay down the rules, but for them to take responsibility for creativity and representation in the cultural field. Sandy Nairne's characterisation of cultural diversity initiatives within British visual arts can be understood in similar terms to that of Lola Young, in which, over the past three decades, arguments had been made within established cultural institutions to extend the parameters of what to fund, strategically develop and programme so as to include Britain's cultural minorities. In both views progress over the period has been gradual and uneven, but their position remained one of the continued need to press for greater equality in all aspects of cultural representation, in employment, artistic programming and in audiences.

From Tate Encounters' analytical position, both Lola Young and Sandy Nairne's contributions interestingly revealed the limits and evident frustration of a conception of cultural politics based upon representation. In this highly established model culture is seen to be made up of identifiable, settled communities, formed along class and ethnic lines of different sizes, shapes, interests and outlooks which through cultural diversity policy can be recognised and acknowledged proportionally by representations and representatives within cultural institutions. In contrast, our research suggests that culture travels along new lines of force, extending beyond the existing institutional boundaries of which the defining feature is that of mobility and transition, involving the spatial, material and virtual.[16] In this view of culture, the challenge is no longer that of achieving fair and proportional systems of representation, but of mapping a new sense of a public realm and acknowledging new kinds of connectedness. In these terms Tate Encounters seriously questions policies aimed at promoting greater inclusiveness based upon a now historical conception of culture. Tate Encounters' rejection of the historical and conceptual basis of cultural diversity initiatives was shared by the third contributor, Munira Mirza.

Munira Mirza saw cultural diversity policy as arising from a 'postmodern' rejection of modernist cultural authority and its continuity with the Enlightenment project. In this she argued that a left/intellectual generation had embraced a cultural relativism, the consequences of which were, proverbially, to throw out the baby with the bathwater. In wanting to challenge the European canon of High Culture, Feminism, Leftism and community arts, academic postmodernism had collectively rejected the transcendental nature of great art. In the process of critique, those responsible for shaping cultural diversity policy lost sight of the fact that culture transcends circumstances and attains an objective and universal condition. For Mirza, cultural relativism's emphasis upon the local and situated nature of cultural reproduction abandoned any universal notion of cultural value. In policy terms, the consequences of these intellectual and political developments have been that culture has become increasingly harnessed to and made to work for political social goals. It follows from Mirza's argument that the instrumentalisation of culture in strategies of targeting Black and ethnic minority artists and communities is the consequence of the intellectual position of cultural relativism. In calling for a rejection of cultural welfarism, Mirza sees the task as one of reasserting the canon and the importance of artistic authority and expertise. For her, cultural policy must find a way of liberating contemporary creativity from the burden of having to be representational.

Tate Encounters' own analytical position also identifies the redundancy of cultural welfarism, but far from aligning this with cultural relativism the view is posed that cultural diversity policy is not relativist enough. There is little to be gained in attempting to revert to the past in an era characterised by its globalising compression of time and space and little usefulness therefore in attempts to restore the particularity of the European canon. Such a view is supported by the research material of Tate Encounters which demonstrates the shifting boundaries and contexts in which the museum experience is subjectively engaged. This would seem to suggest that relativism is precisely a basis upon which to establish future cultural policy.

CHANGING TIMES

Across these three presentations it is possible to see both shared historical conjunctures as well as breaks, which operate along generational, class cultural as well as political lines. It is clear that the development of a British multicultural perspective, which was drawn together and given political and practical expression by Ken Livingstone's leadership of the GLC, was forged by the experience of postwar Caribbean, Bangladeshi and Pakistan migration and settlement in urban city contexts. For Lola Young, it was the children of that first generation, the first generation of Black and Asian Britons whose experience of racism led them, with the British liberal left, to resist and demonstrate against overt as well as implicit forms of racism in their communities and in the institutions of education and culture. As Sandy Nairne acknowledged, his and other white educated liberal's entry into cultural diversity came from the very real politics of a Black and Asian British generation. This, however, is not the generational experience of Munira Mirza, who makes the point that her sense of racial or ethnic identity was of a later and different formation, one in which she sees a counter-cultural politics that rejected the established elitism and adopted instead a 'postmodern' relativism. For Mirza BME categories are racialised and ultimately to be rejected.

There are a number of reasons why Tate Encounters considers that the politics of representation have come to an end, all of which result in the newer recognition that the Internet as well as newer, globalised forms of migration, have radically changed the relations of communities to the idea of nation. The politics of representation of the earlier period rightly problematised the stereotypical nature of dominant cultural representations, pointing out not only the racist basis of Black and Asian representation, but also the invisibility of Black and Asian culture, together with the absence of positive representation. In making these arguments at the level of representation, it was thought possible to create an authentic and collective representation of Black and Asian experience, but in pursuing such a politics of simple authenticity it reproduced its relation to dominant culture and produced a reification of difference. Hard as it was to realise this at the time, and virtually no one did, the politics of the representation of Black, minority ethnic culture could do nothing other than mirror and hence essentialise the racialised subject of the dominant white imagination.

More practically, in terms of an involvement with cultural policies, the politics of representation attached itself, within parliamentary liberal politics, at the limit of its claims for greater equality, which is to say that Black representational politics elided itself with the Labour politics of equal opportunities. In doing this it had to relinquish any claims to a position which would identify the British State as culpable in the machinery of the reproduction of inequality. This was a high price to pay for reforms, especially in the fields of education and culture, that even today remain beyond realisation as already noted.

In the cultural sphere the politics of representation, now coupled with that of the politics of equal opportunities, not only could not challenge the structural reproduction of social inequality but could not mount a challenge to the terms and conditions of competition for equal opportunities either. It was confined to wanting to join the cultural club, to demanding to participate in culture on the terms that dominant culture set. This is the import of Stuart Hall's warning about mainstreaming.

The new critique of the representational politics of multiculturalism is now gathering force and, in Munira Mirza's version of this, the result has been the call to reject the politics of Cultural Welfarism, because it has reproduced a racialised view of culture in the place of a contemporary creative heterogeneity. But the move to replace national representational multiculture with a plea for the universality of creative culture and aesthetic competence and experience is clearly a traditional and conservative move. The claim for the universality of creative culture is the other side of the same coin to the essentialism that claims the authenticity of localised ethnic or racialised cultures. In the end both see culture and its products through highly selective and teleological histories, derived primarily from the binaries of nineteenth-century definitions of art and science in which cultural definition wavers between individual aesthetic experience and anthropological tradition and custom. The current organisation of British public cultural institutions continues in large part to maintain this historical split in which contemporary art is located within the discourse of European Modernism and the history of aesthetics, whilst the rest of the world's cultures, and their diasporic extensions in migrational settlements, remain resolutely contained in the anthropological discourse of heritage.

The central and highly abstract overarching argument of Tate Encounters is that whilst cultural institutions cleave to the aforesaid cultural dualism in order to rationalise their missions and practices, changes in the world and Britain have outstripped the capacity of their binary logic to explain what is currently happening. Whilst the classificatory systems and practical institutional technologies of people and things are all still in place, their explanatory power is near exhaustion. Tate Encounters is not alone in reaching for a model of cultural practice which centrally recognises the transformations taking place in the processes through which cultural value is currently being lived. The concepts which seem to us to have practical utility and reach are some of those derived from those intellectual movements of the 1980s which first began to notice and chart changes in the condition of late modernity. Such changes are centrally associated with what has been labelled as the postmodern and its associated epistemological relativism. Far from seeing the stress on the relative, constructed, situated and particularised nature of culture as the cause of the current confusion, we see it as opening up the space for new ways of configuring and connecting cultural production, reproduction and value from which museums could benefit, if only a move could be made beyond the anxiety of the possible loss of cultural authority. What seems clear from the research is that cultural authority cannot be maintained by a simple insistence on some kind of inherent, fixed and ultimately universal meaning of the objects of collections represented by the stock of historical expert knowledge and validated by custodial practices. The cultural authority of major national cultural institutions is greatly enhanced precisely at moments when they successfully reshape their practices through a grasp of new movements and patterns in cultural production and, equally, when they are able to jettison residual definitions. Far from cultural relativism undermining the pursuit of the best that has been thought and written, it opens the way into a reflexive culture, happy to test all claims and continuously and openly revalue historical culture in the light of present contingent and changing realities.

Keith Piper, (b 1960, Birmingham, England), *Keep Singing (Another Nigger Died Today)*, mixed media, 1982

Art (School) Education and Art History

Leon Wainwright

A DECADE OF DIVERSITY

It seems fair to say that art education and art history have developed throughout the past decade *despite* the demands to attend to cultural diversity. This has been my experience in advocating the need for greater diversity in the art curriculum; I have urged academic practitioners of teaching and learning to address the global relevance of art historical knowledge in the context of an irrefutably diverse world. I imagine that it has also been the experience of those who have resisted the question of 'the global' altogether (however broadly conceived), and for whom diversity issues were never to become a priority. Whichever approach we choose, we are at a complex moment when the terms of diversity in teaching and learning in art and art history seem unprofitable. This appears to be the case regardless of whether we occupy more conservative and reactionary positions, or try to urge radical change. It is a situation that deserves some thought. It may be useful to try and register the changing status of diversity in Higher Education over the recent period, in order to see a way beyond the present circumstances, and what options they present us with.

The immediate post-millennium saw the systematic conjunction of the cultural with diversity. This created a working term that was freighted with suggestions of racial and ethnic difference, so that cultural diversity became synonymous with difference *in toto*. There was a widely enjoined attempt at 'race-ing art history', with a purpose of interrogating or holding up a mirror to art history as a discipline, and to disabuse it of its racism.[1] An often abstract and consequently potent notion of racial difference came centrally into use. Attention to the multiethnic and multiracial, and to race relations, were thus synonymous with the multicultural, cross-cultural, intercultural and transcultural. This went together with the occlusion of the history of art history, of the discipline's role in nation-building and global expansion. From within the rubric of cultural diversity, a litany of new ways was found to describe an underlying, much older interest in essentially ethnicised or racialised modes of encounter, historiography, representation and exchange.[2]

This narrowing and convergence of definitions, the conflation of the cultural field with an unspecified ambivalence about the political fiction of 'race', were no doubt more ideological than critical. Indeed, the problem for diversity became whether this entwining of priorities could last. Was it a suitably analytical term for a more thoroughgoing theorisation of art practices and their histories? Or else nothing more than a strategic one with only a passing usefulness? To embrace cultural diversity in teaching and learning has meant taking up a culturally comparative approach to intellectual inquiry. This is distinguished by being thought capable of resisting the allure of racial essentialism and ethnocentrism. It is an approach to knowledge which is also a scene of important anti-racism.

Even so, the commitment to cultural diversity has coincided with a circumscribed understanding of historical and cultural differences. These are drawn strictly on the grounds of ethnicity and 'race' alone. This is most transparent in academic contexts in art and art history where diversity is invoked, such as in the development of curricula. But here questions of difference are more difficult to broach. Diversity is promoted in a discrete sense, as if somehow removed from the larger and open-ended possibilities for seeing difference as a locus of historical transformation. The result is that a definite mode of particularism has emerged in the primacy of trying to account for diversity. It is to the chagrin of a more dynamic field of inquiry around difference. Certain strictures are placed on those attempting to assume or coin an alternative vocabulary of difference or, more modestly, to simply elaborate on the existing one.

Well before the Equality Bill of 2008, diversity had begun to lose its 'cultural' handle. It has now moved into association with a broader range of differences, including those of age, gender, sexuality, religion or belief, and disability. The assurance of diversity and equality is addressed by integrated working units within Higher Education. They focus on the experience of students and staff largely with regard to areas of admissions, recruitment and pay. They establish protections, such as those against intimidation and workplace bullying. But it is hard to know whether the status of diversity as an institutional priority has grown when coupled with these measures for equality. There is certainly a fear that diversity agendas become somehow diluted through this new association, forced even into a relation of 'competing equalities'.[3] Even so, the art and art history curriculum has not met with an 'equality' agenda on anything like the scale of the agenda for change in the area of cultural diversity. This may be due to the fact that informal policy, such as the Quality Assurance Agency's Benchmarking Statement in the subject area of art and art history, was established before Equality legislation.[4] What would spell disaster for equality is if its anticipated impact on the curriculum were to be gauged against the track record of diversity. There is a popular sense that cultural diversity

– as with multiculturalism more generally – quickly lost the lead in initiatives for change in Higher Education. The emerging challenge is to avoid the pessimism that equality will soon follow suit.

Here I set out some discussion of why I feel cultural diversity should not be seen in this way. I argue why we should not allow diversity to go the way of an early dismissal. It was indeed at one time an expedient term that added institutional value to art and art history education in UK universities, and has since faced resistance. However, it is worth making clear why that description should apply only to the pale institutionalised image of 'cultural diversity' (concomitant with a measurable and managed sphere of differencing). By contrast, what we have not tackled is how to avoid giving up a belief in the recognition for diversity more broadly, and thereby of *misrecognising* difference. We have not questioned why there is an apparent choice between the rising contempt for 'cultural diversity', and yet a closer sense of the 'convivial culture',[5] or ordinary commensality in the cultural life of everyday Britain. What I present, therefore, is not a totalising argument against institutional approaches to difference, nor is it a railing disregard for diversity. It is a case for why we must untangle individual experience from institutional arrangements and to draw out the distinctions between them. We may then see where the study of art and art history may carry us in the light of the recent history of cultural diversity.

GLOBALISING THE CURRICULUM

At the start of this decade I was engaged with a change agenda in the area of diversity, in a national three-year project in curriculum change, 'Globalising Art, Architecture and Design History' (GLAADH), funded by the Higher Education Funding Council for England (HEFCE) under the Fund for the Development of Teaching and Learning.[6] We took as our premise the fact that interest in the global diversity of art, architecture and design history is under-represented in the spaces where it is taught and researched. There was much good teaching practice with relevance to a diverse globalised world, and this had been overlooked in a recent official report.[7] At its inception, the project carried out its own survey of the forty-seven institutions that the report covered and what we found is that little was being done to promote and enhance a breadth of good practice in the area of diversity.

I was with GLAADH for the first half of the project and what I have to say about it is based on my own reflections. It is worth noting initially about GLAADH that 'cultural diversity' was not given any prior definition; members were instead left to set in motion their own sense of the value of the term. On this basis, we chose not to engage in anything like a conventional debate on the meaning of the 'globalising' in the project's title, instead allowing participants to bring their own sense of what the term might mean. During our first year we called for bids from interested departments to become sub-projects of GLAADH, subsequently naming as 'Initiatives' the ten sub-projects who joined until the overall project's end. They were a range of institutions that included the universities of Manchester, Kingston, Glasgow, St Andrews, Aberdeen, Plymouth, Anglia Polytechnic, De Montfort, Birkbeck, Sheffield Hallam, and Central England; a range of old and new and projects of various sizes and ambitions. What they shared was a common aim to integrate 'diverse' materials properly into the curriculum, to embed diversity, and to combat the tendency to relegate them to the status of tokenistic 'ethnic add-ons'.

It is fair to say that the GLAADH project did not lead to the sort of change that I thought we were hoping for. Of course, we could, and we did document evidence of 'impact' on more than a fifth of the AADH community in the HE sector. The project was evaluated externally and thus described; it became a flagship project for the Learning and Teaching Support Network, and a key element in an important phase of the Fund for the Development of Teaching and Learning. But there was a particular obstacle that the project highlighted which suggested that there would continue to be real difficulties and disappointments in establishing a more diverse curriculum. The project never hazarded a definition of diversity exactly, but it is impossible to review its significance without one. So I would suggest that the changed curriculum it aimed for is one that does not operate under the segregations of mainstream versus diverse, or Art versus World Art (and of Art versus Non-Western Art, which was the terminology that we encountered most frequently). It is on this area of divisions, and around the issue of the place of diversity within art history as a whole, that the really significant results of the project show up.

What we had highlighted specifically had more to do with individual academic teaching staff and their self-understanding in relation to the curriculum, than with some larger institutional or policy failing. We repeatedly heard it said, with emphasis, that in order to deliver more global or 'diverse' topics, individuals felt that they had most of all to be 'experts'. This meant someone with an established research specialism in a field identified with 'cultural diversity'. (It was easy to point to my own profile: trained at the School of World Art Studies at East Anglia, and the School of Oriental and African Studies, London, rather than Oxbridge and the Courtauld.)

This is significant for the larger enterprise of change. It is easy to understand why the relation of research to the curriculum should come to be of issue when academic identities tend to be defined by research profiles. However, the cultivation of 'expert' status in the diversity debate probably rests more on what is taking place beyond the academy in the arts and public sectors. There the conjunction of professional identity formation with, in particular, the cultural politics of marginalisation – the growing interest and movement of marginal issues to core issues

– probably underlies the reasons why diversity initiatives in the academic environment have been so diluted. The result in art history is that diverse topics of teaching and research are *ethnicised*; and so are their practitioners, their teachers and researchers, and by extension their students. They are made to appear outside the mainstream of art historical interest, or else included or 'accommodated' on rather dubious terms. Most worrying in all of this is that academics of the notional 'majority ethnicity' (which has not even been seen as an ethnicity at all) have largely dismissed their own potential as agents for change. They have actively self-selected, or else dismissed the potential of one another to bring about change, and so stood in one another's way. They have felt that identifying with a majority ethnicity rather disqualifies the effort to understand marginal positions. This is regarded as an inauthentic path that crosses over into foreign territory. The outcome is that the individual member of academic staff then disengages from diversity matters as if they were someone else's proper domain.

But this of course is to misrecognise what we may mean by diversity. It is worth remembering that conditions for change are over-determined when initiatives are emptied of their legitimacy well in advance of being mobilised. What GLAADH showed is that it is all too easy to lose sight of our own diversity, or else to relocate a sense of diversity to somewhere outside the usual run of our attention – to relate it to other people and other people's business. Our meditations in planning the project were forever focused on a non-prescriptive approach to teaching about difference. I can recall one meeting when the project team members vocalised a sense of their own identities as fractured by difference in various ways: with regard to gender and age, certainly, but we also each hailed from peripheries of one sort or another, whether the hierarchies of British regional, social and ethnic identities, or from outside the Anglophone world. Our coming together and mobilisation of such differences was not by design. It was not aimed at 'managing' diversity to produce in the project a semblance of representativeness. It was the result of true contingencies, of fertile common ground and shared critical interests expressed through and not despite difference.

INCLUSION AND ITS AFTERMATH

Terms such as diaspora and cross-culturalism have entered the teaching of art and art history from their more established place in the social sciences, namely in cultural and media studies. When we teach about migration, diaspora, belonging, national identity, difference and diversity, we have tended to draw liberally on what has been established in these other disciplines. It might be argued that this creates an interdisciplinary space of critical writing about art that enriches all of its participant disciplines. Still, there is cause to wonder whether this separate field of inquiry is not rather too isolated from art historical theories and methods in the main. Certainly many artists – largely those associated with 'cultural diversity' – have come to be studied in disciplines other than art history, or in a separate space within art history away from its central, canonical ground. This disciplinary arrangement has helped to cultivate a complementary or secondary discourse for certain artists alongside mainstream art history.

There is a strand of art and art history teaching that responds to the demand for radical change in the arts that was first championed by critical commentators and artists who had tired of marginality, racial exclusion and 'invisibility'. But those same demands are increasingly part of the package of measures by which techniques of segregation from art history are reproduced. There is a further complication in the present climate. Presenting themselves as suitable subjects for cultural diversity initiatives in public arts funding, artists themselves are often hurriedly complicit with forms of differencing that lead to their separation from art history in the main. This is a sort of self-objectification – a 'xeno-' or 'ethno-spectacle' – in response to the demands of marketplace and public patron. Yet there is a firm contribution to this process by art and art history in the way that the curriculum is constituted to include discrete topics on 'diversity' and in its use of disciplinary tools from elsewhere.

The artist, curator and writer Olu Oguibe has described how:

> At the turn of the twenty-first century, the struggle that non-Western contemporary artists face on the global stage is not Western resistance to difference, as might have been the case in decades past; their most formidable obstacle is Western obsession with an insistence on difference. As some have already pointed out, it is not that any would want to disavow difference, for we are all different one way or another, after all. The point is that this fact of being ought not constitute the crippling predicament that it does for all who have no definite ancestry in Europe.[8]

Oguibe is focused on a new phenomenon, or an old phenomenon seen on an unprecedented scale. It is the inauthentic incorporation of difference – an 'insistence on difference' – in such a way that goes against the interests of those who have been historically excluded from the art market and art history. This has reached the level of 'obsession' as the global art marketplace plays what Oguibe calls its 'culture game'. The 'game' takes place when difference assumes a discrete and stable category, and is consequently accommodated into the commodity system of the art mainstream. It is cultural diversity being traded as currency. Higher Education teaching operates together with patterns of art criticism, curating and arts programming (and indeed, with many artists themselves) to constitute difference as a commodity and in shaping this 'predicament'.

Trying to understand the place of artists and artworks in this process, the cultural theorist Sean Cubitt has written:

> Where once the task was to champion the silenced voices and invisible canvases of artists outside the pale of the power-broking metropolitan galleries, now it is to understand in what ways global art practice has become a spice to flavour the pot of the new multiculturalism.[9]

In what has been described as 'the carnival of hetero-culture now at large in the metropolis',[10] ours is a time when diversity in the teaching of art and art history discloses the operational language and the complexities of Britain's current politics of multiculturalism. In arts programming and the art market appetites have sharpened for ethnic, racial and cultural 'difference and diversity'. It would seem as though the pleas for inclusion from those who are at the historical margins of art history have therefore finally been heard. Even so, the development of such appetites has meant that artists are under increased pressure to provide an explicit codification of accepted forms of difference in their practice. The artist and researcher Sonya Dyer has described in her report on 'artistic autonomy' for the campaign group, The Manifesto Club, 'the unhealthy pressure on artists and curators from non-white backgrounds to privilege their racial background above all else in relation to their practice'.[11] This raises the concern that apparently radical terms of cultural analysis have achieved a more popular embrace without any ensuing substantive change.

We might argue that the need to privilege a 'racial background', as Dyer indicates, in fact hardly features in an art curriculum that 'includes' artists such as Oguibe. There may be scope for studying these artists as a view onto the historical architecture and the legacies of exclusion and marginalisation in the hegemonic spaces of art galleries, museums and historiography. Their presence in the curriculum may not foreground or embody racial difference so much as highlight and undermine racism. Yet even this preferred purpose for such artists may be considered another, if lesser, 'unhealthy pressure' on them. We must ask whether certain artists are also studied in ways that decouple them from the terms of both racism and 'race'. Under the demands for 'cultural diversity' this cannot be so – their presence exemplifies a theme of discourse around cultural or diasporic difference and yet not much more.

The artist, curator and writer Rasheed Araeen has described this situation as a sort of 'tyranny' ensuing from modes of viewership which

> ... have very little to do with the specificity of art and which have now been appropriated by art institutions that use them to reinforce their colonial idea of the Other. This has helped them redefine postcolonial artists as the new Other, but also predetermine their role in modern society. With the result that any art activity which does not conform to or defies this new definition is looked upon as inauthentic and is suppressed.[12]

In Araeen's view such 'postcolonial' artists live and work persistently within the limits set by their viewers, and are forced to negotiate official sources of support and institutionalised practices of art reception. The field of art education intersects with such contexts of reception. In these spaces, concerns about modern and contemporary aesthetic criteria are paid to artworks by and large only when their makers are white. Such criteria are put aside in favour of using the tools of the social sciences, and of cultural and media studies, for the art of 'diverse' practitioners.

In this way, the art curriculum orchestrates evidence of a separate tradition of art-making, an 'Other' to European modernism. This is the teaching and learning arm of the promotion of ethnic or racial difference as expedient in the wider art environment. Certainly the vocabulary of cultural analysis – with attention to the migrant, diasporic and postcolonial – has fully penetrated the study of certain artists, while their exclusion from the mainstream has continued. Those artists who readily identify as diasporic or postcolonial are now placed in a circumscribed space, and kept there with the assistance of the art curriculum. The expectation that such artists make works that are best viewed as cultural evidence of their Otherness has contributed to undermining their value and reinstating ethnic and racial hierarchies.

Such a preference has helped to constitute an unsatisfactory form of inclusion – what elsewhere has been identified as 'differential inclusion'[13] – brokered through academic models drawn from disciplines other than art and art history. This is a reproduction of the existing order, where, as Paul Wood has written, 'the underlying structure (and of course, the wider structure-beyond-the-structure) has remained intact'. Addressing this development over a thirty year period, Wood has noted 'how little has changed' since the time of his writing, with Dave Rushton, the long pamphlet, *The Politics of Art Education*. This comprised a 'radical reportoire' that involved the 'questioning of the authority of the western canon'.[14] With this intractable continuity in view, we might consider what appreciation is being fostered through the curriculum of a deep sense of the transformative and critical potential of art making. It would also be worth asking what future is there for an engaged mode of teaching. The curriculum actively contributes to undermining the very artists who have staged a questioning of canonical knowledge, and who prompted the development towards the recent historical moment of cultural diversity.

SEEING THE WAY TO A REAL DIFFERENCE

An added dimension to debates on difference is brought by the winner of the 2003 Turner Prize, artist Grayson Perry, writing that 'There seems to be a very new Labour idea that if we rigorously ensure a numerically fair proportion of BME (black or minority ethnic) practitioners, then that will automatically facilitate social justice in wider society. Hmm.'[15] The suggestion here is that the multicultural 'mainstreaming' of attention to art is not the same as more widely-reaching social, political and economic change. This assessment tallies with Martha Rosler's description of the situation in the United States during the 1990s, of 'an art world version of multiculturalism (and where more appropriately situated than in the realm of culture?), necessary but sometimes painfully formulaic, which produces a shadow constellation of the identities of the wider society but without the income spread'.[16]

Nowhere is this better exemplified than in the nature of recent attention to the artist Chris Ofili who is firmly within the mainstream of contemporary artists and broadly identified as black (of Nigerian parentage and raised in England). The largely unacknowledged modern and contemporary art history of the Caribbean has not become any more visible since Ofili took up permanent residence on the island of Trinidad in 2005. The opportunity has not been taken for a merging of British and Caribbean horizons and art histories. Outside a few examples of radical historiography, there is no transatlantic, transnational awareness of the art and artists that comprise the Trinidad context of Ofili's current path as a painter.[17] Ofili's promotion follows the pattern of satisfying inclusion in the short-term. It produces a hyper-visibly black, even 'post-black' presence that unfolds without any constitutive change to art history, curating or art education at large. It is the terms of representation in these fields, and what difference the promotion and inclusion of certain artists *cannot make*, which should now concern us the most.

Such perspectives are largely corroborated by current research in the field of cultural policy studies. This has moved away from so-called 'impact analysis', the enterprise to determine the value and function of the arts and of how artworks actually affect people. The preferred direction for this field is, first, to draw back from presenting 'appealing advocacy arguments' that would otherwise be demanded in any account of the positive impact of the arts, and second, to signal 'unexpected and rewarding directions' for research.[18] One direction that has been paid little attention is that of art and art history education, and yet it is unclear why this should be considered so out of bounds for systematic research on the cultural and the social. There are poor results observed both within and beyond the arts of initiatives of cultural diversity and difference. These suggest that the critical use of their vocabularies has not fulfilled the ambitions of historically excluded and marginalised artists. This picture appears to agree with the sense of needing to think beyond the advocacy of marginalised individuals and groups in art history, as if advocacy were somehow part of the wider problem. Cultural policy studies has also sought to expose the wider historical and political background to ideas of a shared or common culture and the notion of social or national unification in the arts. This would illuminate the historical role that the curriculum for art and art history has played in constructing categories of community as well as difference. It may help to show how phenomena such as the art history canon serve to structure the art mainstream, and so inevitably assist in marginalisation and exclusion.

Further to this account of the institutional space of education are some powerful contradictions that would repay the broader inquiry into relations between difference and works of art. They would also suggest not the end of advocacy, but its return in an unexpected way. I wonder whether declarations of the end of advocacy are to do with a loss of political will to see the arts as a suitable setting for struggle, and whether traditions of 'engaged' scholarship, criticism, teaching and learning can and should be so gleefully abandoned. If by advocacy we mean the narrow pursuit of diversity and difference as forms of objectification, the ethnicising of art works, of curricula, students and their teachers, then its lifespan should duly be over. But in negotiating a contrapuntal or counter-hegemonic route, in creating alternatives in the face of the commoditisation of difference, surely we already undertake to advocate.

Such advocacy marks the end to what Sean Cubitt calls the 'belated revolution' of 'the assimilation of the exotic Other into the new world art'.[19] It works to disrupt those practices in which artworks, artists and art histories are promoted under the terms of diversity and multiculturalism; it works to lift the barriers and exclusions that such assimilation represents. Slavoj Žižek has argued that the customary logic behind this incorporation of cultural diversity is in order to create the semblance of a conflict-free space of commerce.[20] The remaining option for any oppositional participant in this setting is to shatter that semblance and to bring on the conflict – a far different role from the one assumed during the promotional drive to diversity.

Grayson Perry embodies an intersection between the performance of sexuality and a polemic on ethnicity. He reminds readers of the need to confound contemporary Britain's political investment in discrete categories of difference. However, the idea that ethnicity may serve as a principal site of difference for the writing and teaching of art history may be disrupted not by the shift from diversity to equality, but by a more 'intersectional' notion of diversity that draws upon the taxonomy of equality. One possibility is that it may come from the locus of teaching and learning in art and art history education itself. This is a clear vantage point for registering a difference in practice despite the wider shifts in programming and policy around the terms of representation.

I am wary of the generation of a separate, if complementary, discourse in this area. So I would prefer to see academic practitioners seizing the opportunity to move contingently as well as in conflict with the unfolding story of cultural diversity. We need express no long term commitment to one or other institutional agenda or vision, yet nor should we pretend to be free of their influence. Shaping a less overdetermined field of intellectual and creative culture demands that we find an elective affinity with those who have felt excluded or marginalised from official spaces. It requires us to see our institutional frames differently. This is not simply about defamiliarising the academic setting for art and art history, but daring to abandon the myths of diversity that have framed our efforts. Ultimately, we need to see our way to a real difference by winning back our own diversity.

Sonia Boyce, (b 1962, London, England), *She Ain't Holding Them Up, She's Holding On (Some English Rose)*, 1986, conté pastel and crayon on paper, 218 x 99 cm, Cleveland County Museum Service

Breaking the Code
New Approaches to Diversity and Equality in the Arts

Hassan Mahamdallie

INTRODUCTION

Expanding equality and democratic possibilities in the realm of arts and culture can take us all – arts institutions, theatres and galleries, arts companies, artists, academics, curators, critics, audiences and participants – on a journey that leaves behind increasingly outmoded approaches to our artistic and cultural life in favour of new ways of seeing and telling and making. We can begin to overcome notions that have wrongly cast diversity and equality policies as an unwelcome obligation or burden on the artistic world, and instead turn this 'deficit model' into its opposite – a progressive force that can renew the arts in this country and lay the foundations for its artistic and democratic renewal.

Arts Council England is committed to developing the creative or artistic case for diversity – that recognises that art placed in the margins through structural barriers and antiquated and exclusive approaches needs to be brought to the centre of our culture and valued accordingly. The Arts Council believes that the creative case approach demands three interlocking progressions:

1 Equality

There has to be a continued drive for equality to remove barriers in the arts world, releasing and realising potential and helping to transform the arts so that they truly reflect the reality of the diverse country that we have become but still do not fully recognise.

2 Recognition

There has to be a new conversation that attempts through various means to resituate diverse artists, both historically and theoretically, at the centre of British art – whether that is the performing arts, the visual arts, music, literature or film.

3 A New Vision

There must also be the construction and dissemination of a new framework for viewing diversity, one that takes it out of a negative or 'deficit' model and places it in an artistic context. Diversity becomes not an optional extra but part of the fabric of our discussions and decisions about how we encourage an energetic, relevant, fearless and challenging artistic culture in England and the wider world.

The belief that there is only one way of defining taste, only one canon by which to judge what is great art and what is not, has increasingly been challenged over the past forty years. In many respects, old fashioned elitist notions of a universalist Western canon have been hollowed out by streams of critical thought that have succeeded, in part, in infiltrating even our biggest arts institutions.

However, those who have the power to define what is 'great art' still give the impression that their judgments are based on 'expertise', following universal rules traced all the way back to the Greeks and the Romans, and that only those who are trained to decipher the code can understand the true intrinsic value of the work of art, the recital or the performance.

So, although there may have been an intellectual tilt towards a more egalitarian view of history and of diverse arts practice, the reins of power, and thus authority, largely remain in the same privileged hands. In a sense a culture of middle-class entitlement still prevails. A significant shift in the access to resources, to galleries and stages and to academic legitimacy has yet to take place.

Also, there are many fields of endeavour that have yet to be fully opened up. For example, there needs to be an appreciation by policy makers and funders that much innovation takes place at the margins, yet it is this experimentation with ways of seeing and telling that reinvigorates culture and connects it to present realities, not those of past times. This is not new thinking: the innovative potential was highlighted in Sir Brian McMaster's 2008 report to the Department of Culture, Media and Sport into excellence in the arts:

> Within these concepts of excellence, innovation and risk-taking, and running through everything that follows below, must be a commitment to diversity. The diverse nature of 21st century Britain is the perfect catalyst for ever greater innovation in culture and I would like to see diversity put at the heart of everything cultural. We live in one of the most diverse societies the world has ever seen, yet this is not reflected in the culture we produce, or in who is producing it. Out of this society, the greatest culture could grow… it is my belief that culture can only be excellent when it is relevant, and thus nothing can be excellent without reflecting the society which produces and experiences it.[1]

We can all be enlightened by new ways of telling the story of the development of contemporary art in Britain. Post World War II immigration has forever changed the essence of British life – so why cannot this be properly articulated within the arts? There needs to be an acknowledgement that, for example, artists whose work has been marginalised through inequalities and structures of discrimination in wider society have nevertheless had a significant and sometimes pivotal influence on artistic genres, forms and styles that have developed over the years. Diversity in its widest sense is intrinsic to the development of art and culture, yet this viewpoint is often obscured by orthodox and dogmatic narratives and histories.

Rasheed Araeen of *Third Text* has already identified a 'missing story' in the context of post Second World War visual arts:

> The presence of artists in Britain originating from Africa, Asia and the Caribbean is totally absent from the official narratives of art history... Although some Afro-Asian artists have been received benevolently and with admiration, there is little institutional recognition that the absence of non-white artists from mainstream art history has falsified the history of modernism.

Similar points can (and have been) been developed around the way in which women artists have been situated in the mainstream discourse. When the artist Louise Bourgeois died recently at the age of ninety-eight, obituary writers and art critics praised her for her 'persistence' and noted that she had not gained deserved prominence until she was into her seventies. However most did not touch on how she was excluded from the charmed circle of male artists whose work was purchased and exhibited by the Museum of Modern Art in New York in the late 1930s:

> Because I was French and kind of discreet, they tolerated me – with my accent I was a little strange, I was not competition – and I was cute, I guess. They took me seriously on a certain level, but they refused to help me professionally. The trustees of the Museum of Modern Art were not interested in a young woman coming from Paris. They were not flattered by her attention. They were not interested in her three children. I was definitely not socially needed then. They wanted male artists, and they wanted male artists who did not say they were married. They wanted male artists who would come alone and be their charming guests. Rothko could be charming. It was a court. And the artist buffoons came to court to entertain, to charm.[2]

It took MoMA fifty years to mount a major exhibition of Bourgeois's work (and thereby the first retrospective of a female artist). According to the artist herself this finally came about in 1982 because a female curator, Deborah Wye, 'convinced them [the trustees] that I was important'.

'DIVERSITY LITE' – INEQUALITY IS STILL THE ISSUE

There has been criticism that often 'diversity' within arts institutions and the wider art world has been confined to specific micro-policies, while the bigger policy and operational areas have failed to integrate equality and diversity into their work. So while institutions can point to their diversity policies, major inequalities in reality may still remain. In fact, diversity is not the problem. Diversity exists; it does not have to be created. The issue is inequality within a diverse society, and diverse arts community, and within its history, its practice and critical debate, some are far more equal than others. This presents the paradox of the creative process, diversity rich in inspiration, but the distribution and consumption of the creative product being delivered in the main through a network of exclusive clubs.

The issues of diversity and equality do need to be integrated into the bigger questions that we face. For example, there needs to be more conscious scrutiny of the economic and infrastructure models that are pursued in the arts and their impact on artistic practice, diversity and creativity. The 'creative cities' model was outlined in the urban studies theorist Richard Florida's book *The Rise of the Creative Class* and has had a profound influence internationally on politicians and town planners seeking to regenerate inner cities.3 One study summarised Florida's argument thus:

> Diverse, tolerant, cool cities do better. Places with more ethnic minorities, gay people and counter-culturalists will attract high skilled professionals, and thus get the best jobs and most dynamic companies. And Florida seems to have sheaves of data to back it all up.[4]

The study goes on to note that:

> Some cities and states are already putting Florida's ideas into practice – Michigan, Cleveland and Philadelphia have all launched 'cool cities' initiatives, for example. In the UK, Liverpool is now considering creating a 'Gay Quarter'. Dundee has zoned a new 'Cultural Quarter' next to the city centre.[5]

Florida argued that cities need economic policies to attract and nurture the 'creative class' that is the dynamic hub of the model. On the face of it, this sounds ideal – urban regeneration built around a concept of diversity. Yet as many observers have pointed out – diversity without increased equality may be seen as no more than 'diversity lite'. Some academics and critics have argued that the meritocracy and coolness of Florida's creative class rests upon continued inequalities at the base of society. Jamie Peck has observed that:

At various points, Florida concedes that the crowding of creatives into gen-trifying neighborhoods might generate inflationary housing-market pres-sures, that not only run the risk of eroding the diversity that the Creative Class craves but, worse still, could smother the fragile ecology of creativity itself. He reminds his readers that they depend on an army of service workers trapped in 'low-end jobs that pay poorly because they are not creative jobs', while pointing soberly to the fact that the most creative places tend also to exhibit the most extensive forms of socio-economic inequality.[6]

Lakhbir Bhandal, a Director of the Change Institute, who has been looking at the connections between diversity, creativity and innovation, puts it this way:

> Florida is saying that people want to live in places that are multicultural and diverse and open to all sorts of people but then he says black people don't benefit in those societies. They create a nice backdrop for the others, without benefiting themselves. It doesn't necessarily follow from diversity that equality results.[7]

The creative class is drawn from the creative industries, which are themselves seen as an important driver for the British economy. Yet it is widely recognised that the creative industries have an ongoing problem with diversifying themselves. Creative and Cultural Skills points out that 'The sector is 95 percent white and 65 percent male.'[8]

An Arts Council commissioned study talked to the student pressure body The Arts Group, revealing:

> In a survey of its graduate members, The Arts Group found that the signifi-cance of contacts and networking was even higher. Kit Friend, the group's communication officer, told us: 'Networking remains the key method – around 80 percent – of finding opportunities, effectively perpetuating closed circles of contacts dominated by the middle classes. As long as there is no properly structured and accessible recruitment path, we will not be able to open up opportunities to those with talent. We appear to be heading quite willingly into a model where those who can afford to pay [by being able to undertake unpaid internships] are able to access the best paths to the crea-tive sector.[9]

An Arts Group study found that sectors that are part of the creative industries ex-hibit structural inequalities which go beyond crude 'head-counts':

> The evidence also points to a clear occupational skewing of BME [Black and Minority Ethnic Community Services]... For example, in the film industry, much BME employment is accounted for at the exhibition and distribution

end of the value chain, whilst BME employees are less likely to hold more senior positions.

It is clearly not the case that Black and Asian creative businesses are ghettoising themselves, and need to pull themselves up by their bootstraps and make more of an effort to break into 'white' networks. The doors must feel shut to them.

DIVERSITY, CREATIVITY AND INNOVATION: WHAT ARE THE LINKS?

All this shows that diversity and equality cannot and should not be de-coupled. But the argument why this relationship is important needs to be properly fleshed out and articulated. In the recent past there have been many and legitimate ways in which those arguing for wider diversity and equality have sought to convince others – a moral case for diversity arising out of the Stephen Lawrence inquiry (it's good for society), an economic case for diversity (it's good for business), a legal case (it's the law), but the creative case (it's good for the arts) remains as yet under-developed. That is not to say that it would be a hard argument to win. We believe that most people connected in the arts 'instinctively' understand that the dynamic between diversity and creativity and innovation lies somewhere at the heart of the artistic act – but where exactly?

Lakhbir Bhandal from the Change Institute argues that we need to put some thought into how diversity and creativity is 'managed' for us to reap the full benefit:

> There is research into getting a heterogeneous team together and seeing if they do better than homogenous teams. They found that yes, there is more creativity in the long run but the process is complicated and difficult to man-age. It's not a given that if you throw a bunch of people together – it's got to be quite carefully managed. If you look at arts institutions, including the Arts Council, it's not that they aren't diverse, but are they getting the best out of people. Is the diversity being mined in an active way? How many people in these organizations are reaching their full potential?[10]

Bhandal found that researchers into this area have advanced the concept that each one of us is carrying different 'knowledge domains' conditioned by our identi-ties and differences. The key is how we recognise and exploit these knowledge domains:

> You can have a mixed gender group but a lot of men dominating, but it doesn't mean that the women don't have anything to offer. Unless someone is creating the conditions and that space for that knowledge to be expressed, it will remain unused.

The question that arises is how we create these optimal conditions in the arts world. Bhandal thinks that efforts by institutions such as the Arts Council have made a start and that an infrastructure of sorts has been created, but now it needs building upon. In plain talk, there is more to do:

> We are still looking at changing institutions and structures and pulling down resources to get more and more people in the game and facilitate them, and to do that you have to prove that it works. No one will argue it's not a good idea but it will remain on paper unless people can see what it's really all about.

Bhandal argues that the arts community is diversifying along with wider society. There is a need to make sure that the different elements are there, but also to create democratic spaces where these elements can meet on a basis of equality:

> There is diversity in the sense that there are different types of arts organizations but still the interface in a way isn't there. The policies haven't been wrong, you need black RFOs, but it's only been half the process. On the one hand you have been creating an infrastructure but the second phase is to bring it together and I think that process has stalled. Black artists can't integrate into those organisations unless they [the organisations] change.[11]

Of course more questions follow – crucially, how is value applied to diversity and creativity? You can measure the number of ideas generated by putting the two elements together, but what is their creative value? In short – is it worth it? Academics are starting to look at this area of work. A recent paper by cultural economists argued that diversity must be measured as a component of intrinsic value, a significant point that collapses the false opposition that has been set up in some quarters between diversity and excellence in the arts:

> In the arts, perhaps above all other fields, diversity is an important requirement. Almost everyone has their own personal conception of good art. So, aside from encouraging experimentation and innovation, diversity is an important economic requirement in its own right. The arts world is as dominated by fashions and establishments as any other public sphere, and it is notoriously easy for struggling talent to be overlooked and minority tastes to be excluded. *The valuation of diversity itself, as an element of rational choice, is an aspect of establishing intrinsic value that is tackled by economics.* But it is entirely consistent with – and should support – artistic autonomy.[12] [my emphasis]

Many artists seeking to relate to 'the big fish' in the subsidised arts sector report that an appreciation of the value of diversity in relation to artistic practice is not fully recognised or taken to heart. One barrier is how artists who offer artistic explorations rooted outside dominant practice find themselves at a disadvantage. This has been the experience of Mehrdad Seyf, the director of performance company 30 Bird Productions:

> Our work is a combination of theatre, performance, visual arts, architecture, informed by where I come from – partly Iran, partly French School, and of course England.
> The Western world is accessible to the rest of the world, we have access to it, but the rest of the world is not as accessible to those in the West. I was told after an experimental show, 'the next piece you do – can you do a plot with a beginning, middle and an end and characters we can recognize?' No, I don't want to do that. The critics are looking for 'content', performances and narrative. They are looking for a cathartic experience, but it's not about that. You can have a powerful experience without catharsis.
> It's not so much the Western canon in itself – but the way in which is it being used, is what needs to be fought.[13]

Seyf finds that he comes sharply up against the vexed question of power. Who has the power, what are they doing with it, are they prepared to share it with others, and how do those with little or no power relate to it? He says:

> The closer you get the big regularly funded companies, the more you have to bastardise your work to make it acceptable. It begs the question if they are not going to cede power to us, how do we create the work that we want, how do we challenge the establishment and have a dialogue with them at the same time?

These barriers force Seyf in one sense to make a virtue of being 'the other':

> You are all outside of it – this outsideness is important, even mentally I think about standing outside looking in, that is the nature of the engagement. Those of us who don't really have a country are never quite 100%. A group of people who you cannot categorise but who have access to so many references. These inbetweeners are increasing. It's the way of the future.

For Seyf diversity is not a formal code of conduct, rather it is preparation for a step into the unknown.

> Diversity is very important, I make sure it's there by choosing the people I work with, not preaching about it. I don't go in saying 'I am the Iranian

director'; I come in and say 'let's create something'. The diversity will come hopefully in ways that surprise me.

BUILDING A TOTAL PICTURE OF THE ARTS: REMOVING THE BLINKERS

The arts world and the institutions that are there to support it need to encourage and resource new attempts through inventive means to resituate diverse artists, both historically and theoretically, at the centre of British art. The task is not to distort or add more falsifications to the burden of history, but to build a total picture of what has gone before – to acknowledge, learn from and build upon all those artists whose contribution has been up to now ignored or downplayed.

This 'total' approach also allows us to re-look at artists whom we consider important and uncover aspects of their lives that the establishment template cannot hold – for example the role of disability in art. If we can open up these commonly neglected areas of inquiry, there is the chance that a proper place can be given to those artists today who are fighting against their work being devalued or being exoticised, and for its true potential to be recognised.

Colin Hambrook, editor of the resource rich Disability Arts Online, argues that discriminatory attitudes towards disabled artists run deep in Western culture, citing the 'virtue' of the body beautiful elevated by the ancient Greeks and Romans and replicated by the Renaissance.[14]

> There is a key issue we still face – if an artist has an impairment and they are open about it, they will be discriminated against, their work won't be valued or seen in the same light as their peers. There can then be an internal suppression – a pushing away of the importance of that aspect of themselves. Historically, disability was much more institutionalised and entrenched. We can see two thousand years of western culture where there has been the ideology of the perfect human with a perfect body and a perfect mind.[15]

This is not to go back into history and tag famous artists as 'disabled', or even to necessarily claim that individuals past or present have been oppressed or faced discrimination because of disablism. Many artists have been impaired. Henri de Toulouse-Lautrec and Frida Kahlo are two examples well-known to the public. However, it is important to understand how their disabilities may have entered their artistic processes. In contemporary times the Turner Prize nominee Yinka Shonibare has explained how the nature of his disability interacted with his artistic development. A 2001 profile of his work revealed that:

> Shonibare's developing intellectual critique was informed by his own experience of physical disability. At the age of nineteen, while doing a founda-

tion course at the Wimbledon School of Art, he contracted a viral infection that left him completely paralyzed for a month and in a wheelchair for three years. Although able to get about, he has impaired mobility, including limited use of his left side.

This, he insists, made him both more determined and more creative as an artist: 'Historically the people who made huge, unbroken modernist paintings, were middle-class white American men. I don't have that physique; I can't make that work. So I fragmented it, in a way which made it both physically manageable and emphasizes the political critique'.[16]

Race, disability and sex discrimination have particular manifestations in the twenty-first century that demand specific strategies and measures to overcome each of them. One thing anti-discrimination measures have in common however is the tendency to equalise relations between everyone. Freedom is indivisible. The same applies in the sphere of the arts.

Theorists argue that innovative approaches generated by disability arts studies generalise outwards to the benefit of us all. So US academic Terry Rowden argues 'disability has a special force as means of rewriting normalizing narratives because it occurs across all social groups and catagories'.[17]

Colin Hambrook is also adamant that some of the innovations pioneered by the disability arts movement reveal new approaches, in ways which by and large we have yet to appreciate. One would be the way in which galleries, seeking to meet the needs of blind people, allow visitors to use senses other that their visual capacity, such as touch, as a means of revealing the nature of works of art on display. A historical example would be the innovation pioneered by the sign language poet and playwright Dot Miles. She argued for a total appreciation of the aesthetics of her work.

The English language (albeit with a slight Welsh accent) was my mother-tongue. My poems are written from the words and music that still sing in my mind. Of recent years, I have tried to blend words with sign-language as closely as lyrics and tunes are blended in song. In such poems, the signs I chose are a vital part of the total effect and to understand my intention the poem should be seen as well as read.[18]

'THAT WHICH IS NOT ARTICULATED DOES NOT EXIST': WHAT THE MAINSTREAM OWES BLACK THEATRE

The Arts Council's Sustained Theatre initiative is a partnership with the black theatre sector established in 2005 to carry out the recommendations of Baroness Lola Young's 'Whose Theatre?' Report on the Sustained Theatre Consultation.[19] One of the recommendations focuses on encouraging accessible black theatre archives and critical debates on the development of black and Asian British theatre. Baroness

Yinka Shonibare, MBE, (b 1962, London, England), *The Sleep of Reason Produces Monsters (Europe)*, 2008, C-print mounted on aluminium, 72 x 49.5 inches, framed: 81.5 x 58 x 2.5 inches, edition of 5. Copyright the artist. Courtesy James Cohan Gallery, New York/Shanghai and Stephen Friedman Gallery, London

Young wrote:

> There is now no excuse for being unaware that the history and the presence
> in Britain of people of African, Asian, Caribbean and East Asian descent
> stretches back over several centuries. Yet, in spite of that long and complex
> set of histories – many of which involve arts and cultural exchange and ap-
> propriation – today's cultural institutions still feel awkward about engaging
> fully with the descendants of those early settlers… The artistic landscape
> has changed due to the magnitude of human effort made by arts practition-
> ers of African, Asian, Caribbean and East Asian descent. But real embedded
> transformation has proved elusive.[20]

Professor Paul Gilroy makes a similar but wider point when he argues that the
arts have a lot to gain by acknowledging the rough 'conviviality' of cross cultural
exchanges that occur at the base of society:

> I want to suggest that largely undetected (and this is a good thing) either by
> governments or media, in ways that actually go back to the legacy of the
> 1970s, migrants, immigrants, their descendents in this country, might be
> revealed to have generated some more positive possibilities than the melan-
> cholic ones. Alongside all those usual tales of crime and racial conflict there
> are some other varieties of interaction here in this city [London] and in other
> cities particularly, that have developed in a more organic way, let's say.
> Our civic life, I think we can say, has been endowed with that vibrant multi-
> culture that won the Olympics, but we don't always value it, they valued it
> at that moment but it was unusual to do so. We certainly don't use that idea,
> or celebrate that development in ways that we should.[21]

We need to be able to pick out pivotal moments when Gilroy's 'conviviality'
produced something unique and enduring. One of Sustained Theatre's successes
has been to help fund playwright Kwame Kwei-Armah's Black Theatre Archive
project. The investigation, based at the National Theatre Studio, has so far uncov-
ered over 400 African, Caribbean and Black British plays premiered in the UK in
the last sixty years. The project is now archiving the scripts and producing audio
recordings of extracts from selected works.[22]

Kwei-Armah is aware of the dangers of rendering the contribution of black
dramatists invisible, and of the need to resituate key figures and movements inside
the mainstream of British theatre. He warns

> that which is not articulated does not exist – we have been really bad at ar-
> ticulating the links between what could be seen as a peripheral activity and
> its impact on the mainstream.

He gives an example from his own experience:

> Mike Leigh told me he wrote *Two Thousand Years* (2005) after seeing my
> play Elmina's Kitchen (2003) but transformed it from being a black family
> into a Jewish one. How many other artists of stature have been to see black
> plays and narratives that have gone on to inspire their own art? I think there
> is proof of that. Even though we are small in numbers we punch well above
> our weight, and in ways that are far bigger than you recognize. Academics
> should be measuring that and putting it into the mix.[23]

To make the point Kwei-Armah picks out the centrality of the work of playwright
Barry Reckord to the course of postwar British Theatre. Reckord came from Jamaica in the 1950s to study at Cambridge. His first play, written at university, entitled *Flesh to a Tiger*, was staged at the Royal Court in 1958,[24] followed in 1960 by
You in Your Small Corner.[25] Reckord's contemporaries included Caryl Churchill,
Edward Bond, John Arden and Arnold Wesker. Ann Jellicoe, who wrote *The Knack*,
directed *Skyvers*, Reckord's 1963 seminal portrayal of alienated and brutalised
white working class schoolboys up against the authorities.

Or was it? The play's central figure, Cragge, was played by David Hemming in
the Royal Court premiere.[26] All of the characters in *Skyvers* are white. Yet originally
Reckord conceived the play as having black protagonists, but apparently black actors could not be found to fill the roles. So *Skyvers* was adapted to a white working
class narrative instead.[27]

As it stood, *Guardian* theatre critic Michael Billington described *Skyvers* as

> a devastating account by a young Jamaican writer of life in what would now
> be called a 'bog-standard' London comprehensive. Other dramatists, such as
> Nigel Williams in *Class Enemy*, went on to explore the failure of the system
> to cope with those at the bottom of the heap. But Reckord got there first.[28]

Skyvers had a huge impact at the time, but is now largely forgotten, and certainly
has not entered the British theatre repertoire, unlike Bond, Churchill and even
Wesker's work. However Kwei-Armah reports that

> the first play that David Hare saw at the Royal Court was *Skyvers*. Hare told
> me that 'I can't tell you the influence it had on me.' This is our state of the
> nation playwright seeing Skyvers and thinking 'Wow – this is what I want
> to do'.

Reckord played a key role in driving forward British theatre of the 1960s, showing
a way – through heightened language – towards an authentic portrayal of work-

ing class consciousness. But mostly we are a long way from acknowledging and expressing such an integrated vision of key moments that switched the tracks. Kwei-Armah decries the status quo in which

> 'white' work is universal and to be preserved, whereas our work is only instrumental, to be shown once and then thrown away. That is a tenet of racism. Black plays can be universal and socially specific at the same time.

He makes the wider point that to gain authenticity those writers wanting to describe working class experience learned to see through 'a black lens'. From his research Kwei-Armah pinpoints the 1980s as the most influential period of black theatre in Britain:

> The socially political work of the Black Theatre Co-op, Temba, Talawa and those companies firing in the early 1980s – they were big works. They not only employed the leading writers of the day – Farrukh Dhondy and Michael Abbensetts – but they were also training the best directors and designers, who are working today in the mainstream... A lot of guys who are now part of the establishment and honoured were taking a lot from black theatre at the time.

The Royal Court production of Barry Reckord's *Skyvers* with David Hemmings as Cragge (right), directed by Ann Jellicoe 1963, © Photographer Roger Mayne, Royal Court Theatre; image: Theatre Collection/V&A Images, Victoria and Albert Museum.

Playwright David Edgar acknowledged this viewpoint when he said of the role of Black and Asian theatre in Britain that 'Taken as a whole... this canon adds up to a considerable intervention in British theatre, and provides a particular and perhaps unique picture of the making of multicultural Britain.'[29] This creative and innovative exploration of the tensions of inner city life, accessed through a 'black lens' can be identified in the currents running through the best playwrights emerging today. Kwei-Armah uses the example of contemporary playwright Ché Walker to make his point:

> If today I look at writers like Ché Walker, white writers who are choosing to use what I would call black techniques for their rather cutting edge work – using Hip Hop rhythms and Hip Hop narratives and attitudes as a defining factor in their dialogue exchanges and how they construct narratives. Ché is a wonderful example of that, using a black idiom to look at the white working class experience. Diversity is absolutely integral to the voice in his plays.[30]

WHY ARE THERE NO GREAT WOMEN ARTISTS?

At the start of the new millennium the art historian and critic Dr Alicia Foster was asked by the Tate to write a book on women artists. Foster conducted an audit of the Tate collection and found that women made up just fewer than eleven per cent of the artists represented in the Tate (there were 316 women and circa 2600 men) and their work only represented around seven percent of the collection.[31]
Foster was then told that,

> the Tate's position on gender equality was that the collection was just a 'natural' reflection of art history, and that the situation would change naturally, therefore, as women became important artists in greater numbers, that no specific effort needed to be made... I was also told – and it seemed a complete contradiction – that although the statistics I had found might well be accurate, and that the criticism of the museum that they instigated might well be merited, it was not in Tate's interests to make my findings public.

So were there (few or) no 'great' women artists in art history? In 1971 Linda Nochlin wrote a path-breaking essay addressing just this question. Was it, as the art establishment seemed to infer, because 'women are incapable of greatness'?[32] Nochlin's essay was a wide-ranging forensic dismantling of 'the entire romantic, elitist, individual-glorifying, and monograph-producing substructure upon which the profession of art history is based'.[33] The idea that the subordinate position of women in the arts was a natural state of affairs, Nochlin argued, betrayed an intellectual flaw:

In the field of art history, the white Western male viewpoint, unconsciously accepted as the viewpoint of the art historian, may – and does – prove to be inadequate not merely on moral and ethical grounds, or because it is elitist, but on purely intellectual ones.[34]

Nochlin concluded that:

Using as a vantage point their situation as underdogs in the realm of gran-deur, and outsiders in that of ideology, women can reveal institutional and intellectual weaknesses in general, and, at the same time that they destroy false consciousness, take part in the creation of institutions in which clear thought – and true greatness – are challenges open to anyone, man or woman, courageous enough to take the necessary risk, the leap into the unknown.[35]

Why Have There Been No Great Women Artists? set in motion a new area of study of art history, complementing developing theories in the arena of black and colonial struggles. These challenges to the status quo have made substantial headway in the intervening years. However in a 2006 interview Nochlin argued that

since I wrote Why Have There Been No Great Women Artists?, many things changed, but we should still be focused and work on equality between men and women, and challenge what equality means in various places and vari-ous movements.36

The cultural theorist Janet Wolff has argued that in the field of the visual arts there is still a job to do in uncovering women artists in history and analysing their work. But there is also much work to do in challenging the 'natural' view of the artistic legacy that is deposited in museums and galleries:

We should also look at questions about gender made more visible and more central by new theories and by our changed circumstances. The answer to male domination of the museums is not to get rid of all early twentieth century Modernist paintings of female nudes – they are wonderful works of art after all. Instead we should try and figure out new and critical display strategies based, for instance, on juxtapositions which would dismantle the concept of a woman as a passive object of the gaze. Raising a challenging question doesn't have to abolish the pleasure of looking.[37]

Alicia Foster also argues that the conclusion is not to replace one orthodoxy with another.

Instead what's required is an active challenge to the narrowness of past ideas of who makes culture and what forms it might take, married to an openness

to the best of what's being made now in its full variety and complexity...
In terms of the area I work in, therefore, I don't argue for a special type of
'women's art', but for support and recognition of the best art, the best culture
made by women in the broadest sense.[38]

CONCLUSION

The thrust of this article is that future developments in the arts have to go beyond
lip-service to vague commitments to diversity. That is especially important in an
era where we face severe cuts to public spending. It would be a gross error for the
arts to turn inwards, to 'preserve' the status quo. In fact, we would argue that now is
the time to be bold, to acknowledge that those who we think of being at the margins
are in fact, in many ways, the pioneers running in front of us – showing us a different, richer, more dynamic and relevant future for the arts and wider culture.

The Arts Council wants to gather together a consensus that agrees that the relationship between the arts and diversity and equality needs to find another, more
fundamental axis to turn on. The Arts Council certainly does not have all the answers to the questions that a creative approach to diversity and equality throws up,
but it does want to create the opportunities for people to ask profound questions, to
debate them and provide convincing evidence for their assertions and viewpoints.
We hope as a result that the arts community will come to regard diversity and equality as wholly integrated into its everyday thought and practice.

Ten years ago Rasheed Araeen put it to the Arts Council that the presence of artists of African and Asian origin in this country, and their historical achievements,

> was a gift to this society's struggle to come to terms with its postcolonial re-
> alities. It was a gift which was meant to enable this society to re-define itself
> and achieve a new identity... The gift it still there, waiting for this society
> to recognize and accept.[39]

If we are wise enough to accept this gift, and all that goes with it, we have a
chance to transform the relationship between diversity, equality, creativity and arts
innovation, and by so doing set in motion far-reaching changes.

Sutapa Biswas, *Housewives with Steak-Knives*, 1985, oil, acrylic, and pastel on paper, mounted on canvas, 95 x 108 inches, collection of Bradford Museums and Galleries

CONCLUSION
What is to be Done?

Richard Appignanesi

There cannot be a 'conclusion' to this Report in the proper light of its spirit. The Report has premised the idea of a new history yet to be made in the conscious realisation of a culturally integrated future. That future is not distant but could actually be realised in the present, here and now, if we began to perceive the art history of Britain differently. We are at the stage where this radical shift of historical perspective still remains a vision for the practical work to be done.

How the *Third Text* Report came to be commissioned is itself a jigsaw piece of that 'history in the making'. Some time at the end of 2008 we received a call from Hassan Mahamdallie, Senior Strategy Officer at the Arts Council England, which resulted in our first meeting with and him and Tony Panayiotou, Director of Diversity, Arts Council England. They expressed their admiration for our work at *Third Text*, first of all, and eventually said that they wanted to re-frame diversity and equality policies in a way that would put them at the centre of the conversations about the arts. Could we examine that possibility and develop a radical alternative to currently existing cultural diversity policy?

Our Report appears at a seemingly unpropitious moment of 'cultural recession' in British history. But perhaps it can be the opportune wake-up call we needed, all of us in the artworld – artists, critics, art theorists, curators, arts administrators, and especially the art institutions – to shed entrenched compartmental habits of suspicion and see with enlightenment what we must do together to form unprecedented partnerships or wither away in dignified blindness. It is up to us to act in concert against the liabilities of public sector arts funding, always, let it be recalled, even in better times, stringent, and now threatening famine.

Our *Third Text* Report has been designed to address a specific problem, the astigmatism of cultural diversity as a state sanctioned policy, and to offer, so to speak, an ophthalmic correction of that distorted cultural perception. This is what we mean by 'going beyond cultural diversity', seeing past its obstacle to vision, but not in the sense of supplying a prescription for all the ills besetting cultural endeavours or as a ready-made blueprint of the future. Our recommendations are limited to a primary focus on surpassing cultural diversity and, as a consequence of clearing this terrain, identifying some of the complexities that will arise and require consensus solutions. The following ten-point exploratory programme is an invitation to further scholarly research and a platform for public debate.

1 WRITING THE MISSING HISTORY

We must begin from what Chris Smith has called 'a missing history'. And what is glaringly missing in the institutions of art and art teaching is a mainstream history that recognises how and why and what the work of Asian, African Caribbean and African artists has contributed to that history. Chris Smith, former Secretary of State for Culture, and now Lord Smith, was concerned about that 'missing history' because it disables society from ever defining itself as an integrated whole. It is worth repeating here what Smith also said in 1999: 'Without a recorded history, nothing else can follow: no celebration of achievement; not development of a common cultural heritage. This results in immigrant populations looking outside these shores for their history and cultural points of reference.'

We presently have two separate histories of white and non-white artists. While the former is institutionally privileged and seen as fundamental to art historical genealogy, the latter is ignored – as if it had nothing to do with British history – or sometimes referred to as a complementary material (as part of 'cultural diversity'). The institutional priority should now be to bring these two histories together in one integrated narrative in a single book or series of them with a broadly public educational aim in view.

The first to be produced, with an eye to the urgency of this project, must be a scholarly, thoroughly researched volume, and the first of its kind that will give us a fully inclusive account of the achievements gained by the existence of culturally diverse artists in postwar Britain. This book will be a model for ongoing art historical research. Moreover, and crucially, these histories will be aligned to archive-rich research materials, collections of which are already advancing at Tate Britain, other institutions, and indeed including Third Text's own archive.

2 TOWARDS A PUBLIC ART EDUCATION PROGRAMME

We say a series of books, and by this we mean also producing accessible ones for secondary schools across Britain, aimed not only at our many ethnically diverse inner city comprehensives but all of them as equally involved in educating the future members of an integrated society with a shared British heritage. And, of course, not only books but art history workshops should be programmed to acquaint the young with the culturally diverse knowledge production embedded in art history. We cannot stress enough how important it is to begin at the earliest age with a culturally inclusive view of society, with a wide horizon of knowledge, and a basic philosophy that can embrace the world with open-minded wonder. This is not simply 'art appreciation' but a profoundly invested exercise in civic imagination.

We recommend that artists, art historians and educationalists work jointly with the art institutions to coordinate the production of these books and allied programmes for secondary schools, university undergraduates and art students, and that they act in union to secure government funding for this essential enterprise which bears the seeds of a future cultural renaissance.

3 THE FUTURE OF HIGHER EDUCATION ARTS DEGREES, VISUAL AND PERFORMING ARTS SCHOOLS

What are art schools and colleges for? Is it simply for producing more artists? A dubious answer, since it is now seems likely that contemporary Britain has overproduced under-educated art graduates, often technically unaccomplished, ignorant of the basic art historical vocabulary, and at the mercy of a cynical global art market in which the commodification of art prevails. The same criticism may be levelled at performing arts courses with the lesser equivalent of the commercial arts market being the pull of television and Hollywood. There is an evident sense of crisis in our art schools today which stems from their loss of historical direction and resultant lack of credible answer to the question, 'What is an art student being educated for?'

Thierry de Duve, historian, art theorist and curator, has some interesting thoughts on the shape of contemporary art schools. He begins by asking:

> How is art in a given society transmitted from one generation to another? Art schools have not always existed, and nothing says that they must always exist. In a way, they already no longer exist. Their proliferation is perhaps a trompe l'oeil, masking the fact that the transmission of art today from artist to artist is very far from occurring directly in schools. On the contrary, it travels through extremely complex channels that end up implicating the collective as a whole.[1]

The art school, he remarks, 'is a professional school in a very paradoxical sense, since it specifically addresses the young men and women whose vocation destines them to address everyone'. Art, in his view, aims for the 'specific transfer of universal address' to plural publics. And we would agree with his idea: 'Addressing the Other is what distinguishes a work of art.'[2]

It is not the immediate task of this Report to pronounce on the future planning of art schools – or foresee them dismantled in some as yet unimagined re-direction of their goals. But, for certain, a radical change in their vision must come. Our recommendation is that a change of vision in art schools should begin with an integrated language of art and performance history. Art education in Britain, as in other European countries and in America, is still based on the primacy of Eurocentric art and performance history that exclusively celebrates the achievements of white artists. The congruence of cultural diversity in art practice and art history, such as we propose, will restructure our ideas both of the *transmission* of art from one set of artists to another across the generations and the *dissemination* of that knowledge – that 'social capital' as it has been called – to the various publics that compose an integrated collective.

4 CHANGING INSTITUTIONAL ATTITUDES AND HABITS

It is a mere truism that institutions are a composite of the attitudes, habits, skills and career aspiration of the individuals who function hierarchically within them. It is also a truism that institutions tend to reform, for better or worse, from within. No doubt they are subject to change by exogenous pressures – hard knocks from the outside – but, like the civil service, that supreme model of all institutions, they seem to aim principally at their own conservative longevity, and they change 'not so you'd notice'.

Institutions have the well-known effect of institutionalising their personnel and of making the individual corporate. We have noted Andrea Fraser's melancholy insight that, for professionals trapped in the institutional field, 'the institution is inside you, and we can't get outside of ourselves'.

Is institutional change therefore unlikely, unrealistic or downright impossible?

Our Report has achieved at least this glimpse of genuine desire for change, and a serious intent to promote change, from within the institutions. *Third Text* did not embark alone on this Report. It was commissioned by senior officers of the Arts Council, it includes their written contributions and the participation of a Tate official, several academics and a heritage consultant – all of then institutional professionals who would not deny their commitment to career aspirations. What matters is not the apparent few recruits from the institutions present in these pages but the clue they give to the concord of many more such professionals seeking a change of air in their various institutions, and we could indeed say there is a reckoning wind of change now circulating further up the hierarchical ladder.

Our specific contribution at *Third Text* has always been the understanding that positive change is impossible if those in a position to implement it are not in possession of a critical perspective, a philosophy that springs from reflections on genuine knowledge, of a globally inclusive vision of history. The point of this Report is to arm the institutional reformers with a vision of a properly integrated narrative of modern art in Britain, to have it institutionally recognised and disseminated as the true history of British achievement in art. This would provide a foundation, both materially and conceptually, for the prerequisite fundamental change in the current art institutional perceptions and structures.

5 WHAT IS THE ROLE OF CURATORSHIP IN CULTURAL DIVERSITY?

'It is now widely accepted that the art history of the second half of the twentieth century is no longer a history of artworks, but a history of exhibitions.'[3] This is an astonishing statement. One would like to ask who 'widely accepts' it as true? And what does it assume is true of contemporary art? It must have some weight of acceptance, because, if we can refer to Thierry de Duve again, he communicates the apparent consensus that we are living in a society in which

> the diffusion of living art is shared in more or less equal parts between museums and centers of contemporary art in the public sector, along with art galleries and foundations that are products of the private sector but make art accessible to all.[4]

And what he also believes true of contemporary art is that the 'aesthetic aspects of artistic apprenticeship' have been taken over by museums, art centres and galleries. What does this mean?

It means two things with interrelated consequences: first, that curatorship, as an authorial practice, has itself become a form of art; second, that contemporary art is literally being instituted by the curatorial programmes of museums and other exhibition centres devised for entertaining the public in the guise of art historical education. Visitors to exhibition spectacles nowadays are likely to feel muddled by the mix-and-match influence of past 'world art', often designating culturally diverse ethnic artefacts, and the latest fad in neo-avant-garde contemporary art. We are witness to a recycling of history at once backwards to the vestiges of cultural expression, whether of pre-modern Europe or of so-called native peoples of non-European origins, and fast forward to our present consumerist condition. The effect of it is the reverse of what one might expect: the present is exoticised and history comes to a standstill as one more stimulus to contemporary novelty.

If the claims made for curatorship are true, and there is clearly much supporting evidence in operation, then it is equally clear that curators, whether as independent exhibition entrepreneurs, or as museum functionaries, or as artists who now frequently take on the role of curator, bear a heavy educational responsibility. Our task in this Report is to put openly in view the underpinning ideological assumptions by which the artworld institutions structure the public perception of history. The word itself exhibition, deriving from the Latin, ex-habere, 'to hold forth', tells us what should be made manifest, seen, and given to satisfy knowledge. The first small step we recommend is in reality a big one towards 'holding forth' the truth of cultural diversity in the history of art practices. Exhibitions that shift perceptions away from whites-only Eurocentrality to a complete picture of modernism's history in Britain and elsewhere will have a radical effect on the whole artworld and particularly on the public sector of museums and art galleries. The world no longer comprises isolated nation states, incommunicably distant from each other, but is in constant vital dialogue that produces art within a common history. Exhibitions reflective of that contemporary state of affairs will show us what Britain has already achieved as a multiracial society and also lead the way as an inclusive historical model for other countries to follow.

6 ARTS FUNDING IN RECESSIONARY TIMES

It was an ecological disaster waiting to happen. And it did, 20 April 2010. An explosion on BP's Deepwater Horizon drilling rig released a massive, unstoppable oil spillage into the Gulf of Mexico.

Tate Britain's glamorous summer party, celebrating twenty years of BP sponsorship on the Monday evening of 28 June 2010, was disrupted by a small number of artist-activists. Guests arriving at the Tate entrance were harangued by 'Art Not Oil' protesters and five gallons of molasses – resembling a crude oil spill – mixed with feathers were poured down the gallery steps.[5]

The irony or paradox is that these artist-activists have been recipients of Arts Council funding. And why had it taken them twenty years to notice BP's sponsorship of Tate Britain? Or is it because BP and all other corporate sponsors of art are finally seen as involved in some alternative form of money laundering, so to speak, in attempts to 'green' themselves? Is it the real deep water moral issue that art must strive to produce a vision of reality uncontaminated by corporate or state patronage? But that would be called naive. Art has been subsidised under questionable conditions for thousands of years, since Babylon, Egypt, ancient Greece and Rome, right up to the present.

There is no 'moral fact' that can support the uncontaminated autonomy of art. Nor are realistic means at hand to replace subsidy. The trouble is, realism stands perilously close to resignation that can tip over into cynicism, and especially now that our government is introducing us to a 'belt-tightening' regimen. 'Arts told to adopt US-style funding', proclaims the headline to a front page article in the *Financial Times*, 10 July 2010.

> [...a Treasury spokesman said] Most departments have been asked to plan on the basis of 25 to 40 per cent real reductions in spending over a 4-year period...

George Osborne, the chancellor, and Jeremy Hunt, the culture secretary, met leading figures from institutions such as the British Museum, the National Theatre and the National Gallery on Thursday to spell out the consequences of these cuts, although they did not give detailed figures.

One participant said that Mr Hunt told the gathering that the institutions should embrace the US fundraising model which overwhelmingly relies on philanthropic sources and corporate money rather than public funds.

A rejoinder to government policy came from Mark Pemberton, Director, Association of British Orchestras, in the *Financial Times* letters column, 13 July 2010.

Only massive endowments can form a genuine alternative to public subsidy, and as Mr Hunt admitted in his speech to arts leaders at the Roundhouse in London on May 19, endowments take at least 30 years to build. And recent experience in the US shows the danger of an over-reliance on endowments in a volatile market, with serious declines in capital values and yields. In addition, gifts to charities are tax deductible in the US, unlike the UK's Gift Aid scheme, which offer modest tax benefits for higher taxpayers only.

Sir Nicholas Serota, Director of the Tate, also joined in the protest against government cuts to the arts subsidies. He reminds the government that: 'Tourism is our fifth biggest industry; at £20 billion, heritage tourism alone is worth more than the car industry.'[6] Museums and theatres feed vitally into this tourism sector; but there is far more at stake in the 'creative and cultural industries'. 'The public sector provides the training, the research and development, and the chance to experiment that make British culture an international export. We put the creative in the creative industries, and together we are as important to this country as the financial sector. Now it seems that we might be about to throw it all away.' Serota ends with a sombre and prophetic turn of phrase: 'Before the election, the Secretary of State for Culture, Jeremy Hunt, said: "It is actually in recessions that people need art the most." Now there is a danger that we shall produce a cultural recession of our own.'

Are we about to plunge into 'cultural recession'? The effects would indeed be devastating to the reserves of social capital built up in British art from the postwar to the present. What can be done now to shore up this social and culturally diverse capital? The works of Aubrey Williams, Uzo Egonu and many other artists of various ethnic origins mentioned in these pages who contributed to modern art in postwar Britain are still available at modest prices. It is our recommendation that the public art institutions, and Tate Britain in particular, should at once purchase all such works at a fair price from the artists' estates and thereby achieve three desiderata: their rescue from neglect or loss, their protection against the vagaries of art market forces, and most important of all to see them finally installed as the British people's heritage.

Funding must be secured for this enterprise, even in our budget-squeezed recession, because this is not an auction-house speculation in art but a cultural investment whose true value can only realised by the long term effects of knowledge production on our society. We are convinced that a practical plan to schedule the adequate budgetary funding of this project over a number of years is entirely possible, if the art institutions are willing to show foresight and invest themselves in the programme.

7 A MODEST PROPOSAL FOR INFLUENCING GOVERNMENT ARTS POLICY

Can anyone explain this patent absurdity? The Department of Culture, Media and Sport. What sort of barbarism lumps indifferently together 'culture, media and sport'? No mention of art. Does it fit under culture, or media – or perhaps even sport? Or is art the proverbially supernumerary kitchen sink thrown in for good measure somewhere or other?

It would be far better, or at least more honest, to a have a single Department of Culture Industries, since this present Coalition government (and the Labour one before it) clearly views art as a luxury service industry. We have heard its enlightened instruction: 'adopt US-style funding'. Perhaps the arts sector of the cultural industries should adopt another US-style form of leverage, namely the manoeuvres of lobbying as a genuinely potent and fearsome political force. Of course, we know, US lobbies get their enthralling power from the capacity to deliver or withdraw significant blocks of votes that can make or break the party politicians who depend on them not only for re-election and funding but for the everyday routine practices of getting things done. US-style lobbies are owed power. What significant power is owed to the arts sector? None at all, generally, and even those performing arts that enjoy corporate patronage and the largest slices of state subvention, the ones best able to account for some profitable inputs to the culture industry and therefore the Treasury, even they are reduced to proffering advice to the DCMS decision- and policy-makers but cannot seriously influence the political process.

If the chief executive officers of our arts institutions have little political lobbying power, what chance do artists stand of forming a lobby able to influence government policy? An artists' lobby is in any case well nigh unimaginable. Artists do not naturally coalesce, nor are they apt to unionise, and although modern artists seem often to form manifesto groups under some ism or other, or join in a school or movement, these have been ad hoc instances of collectives, political on occasion, such as the Art Workers' Coalition in America, but with a specific target agenda, and usually short-lived.

Art is in the first place an unprotected profession because artistic labour is sui generis and unlike that of industrial or other service industry employees who can withdraw theirs from the workplace in a concerted strike action which will have effect on the employer's decisions. Artistic labour does not have a productive price that can be measured by an industrial output of marketable goods with a per unit profit. The artist has no control on the market price of artworks, insanely high for some, little or nothing for others, because artworks are not strictly commodities, and the artist has no wage-bargaining power that unions can use to negotiate with employers. Art has no use value, in Marx's terms, but is a purely imaginary deposit of surplus value realisable only in cultural evolution.

Leonardo could possibly have downed tools and refused to complete the Mona Lisa. His patron would be sorely displeased, but we cannot see any socio-economic consequences to Leonardo's strike action – except to have deprived the future of a masterpiece.

It is here, in this unimaginable gap in the future where the Mona Lisa should have been but isn't because the artist withdrew his labour from its existence, that we can suggest a modest proposal for influencing government arts policy. What is irreparably lost to the future by damaging the public sector, identified by Serota as 'publicly supported activity' which provides 'the training, the research and development, and the chance to experiment', and that we in this Report have emphasised time and again as the knowledge production springing from culturally diverse art practice? It would be gravely irresponsible to sit by and watch our social capital leached away from the future to finance this moment of wilful politically imposed cultural recession. Let us be clear. It is a political decision that commands those cheated by the recession to pay for it. Our government, Coalition or Labour, seems determined that the dealers in financial chicanery who caused the recession, who preyed on the naive credit hungry public, must be restored to their former unassailable status.

How will art cope with that kind of governing realists?

Our proposal requires farsighted partnership alliances between artists and the executives of art institutions, between those who are the most imaginative, who possess the most advanced knowledge of cultural diversity in art practice on a global scale, the most politically astute who can tirelessly and relentlessly lobby our present or any subsequent government that persists in wearing the emperor's new clothes of recession. Lobby them for what? For sustained public sector investment in the arts.

Is it possible? It is entirely possible.

8 THE FUTURE OF ETHNIC COMMUNITY ORGANISATIONS

The present government sponsored and Arts Council funded ethnically based community organisations should not be regarded as exclusively specific ethnic cultural sites, but open to the needs of the whole community regardless of ethnic origins, and enabled to share their particular experience of diversity with others from different cultural backgrounds.

The point has been made before and is worth repeating here. Traditional ethnic crafts and cultural expressions are fine as such, and there is room for them in an integrated society, but there must be no policy expectation that they constitute the sole boundaries within which contemporary artists of Asian, Caribbean or African origins are obliged to operate. What is expected of these culturally diverse artists is that they bring their experience to bear on contemporary art but not necessarily to express themselves only within the confines of past traditional means.

9 HEARING THE SILENCED

The ethnic minority communities of Britain have achieved a voice to which the state must pay some heed. It could be argued that an official policy of cultural diversity – mistaken as we see it – would not be in place if the state did not acknowledge and to an extent fear that voice.

But who speaks for the poorest white sector of the British population, by no means an insignificant minority, or even suspect it of any voice worth heeding? Perhaps, God help us, the British National Party? Fortunately not. Britain's deprived whites have confounded any expectation that sheer despairing anger at the chronic neglect of their plight would drive them into the embrace of rightwing extremism. They appear by their resounding silence deaf to the BNP's claims of white supremacy. Is it because deprivation leaves one apathetically disinclined towards politics of any sort? Or do these folk know something that has eluded the BNP and the privileged rest of us? Perhaps the answer is, yes, they do, which is not to confuse race with class antagonism, a wisdom that has apparently gone out of fashion in the other sectors of society. No one to our knowledge has much bothered to research the real whys and wherefores of their views, nor consider their aspirations which they are presumed not to have.

An exclusionist terminology, every bit as pernicious as that inflicted on the ethnic minorities, has been applied to them: 'terminally unemployable', benefit scroungers', 'sink estate denizens', and most injuriously, 'white trash'. Our vote-greedy politicians have been reprehensible in dismissing these citizens as politically weightless – a sort of post-industrial detritus that can be swept out of sight and mind. These residues of the *dis*-employed are not only inner city dwellers but are found in the scatterings of gutted mining and rural communities.

Where is the government funding for community organisations aimed at their needs? What are the measures envisaged for their cultural integration and participation in an equitable society? What, and more to the point, where is their 'heritage' in a society that has no place for them? Our faith in a genuinely integral but diverse British culture expressed in this Report would be mere 'tinkling brass', in the words of St Paul, if this situation is allowed to continue without foreseeable remedy.

What is to be done? What cannot be done is to speak for them – or even to speak of 'them' in such reductive anonymity as the 'others' in our midst. Our recommendation is in the first place to acknowledge the silenced who are the segregated outcasts within our shores, and then to agree on the practical integrational steps, educational, cultural and social to rectify the injustice.

What we are to do should never tempt us to perceive others as disabled. We must beware of causing affront to non-white and socially disadvantaged people by confusing the issues of cultural diversity and disability. The problems of cultural diversity are not due to the 'disability' of so-called 'ethnic minority' or other communities but of the system itself which sees them in need of help to overcome their 'handicap'. A perception of that kind is tantamount to racism and ought to be considered an institutional disability stemming from the legacy of colonially motivated segregationist thinking.

Change will come when the equality of all people is recognised within a common framework and history. A desirable conclusion, no doubt, but the mere expectation of change will not resolve the issue of disability. For how much longer must the disabled citizens of Britain tolerate their condition of 'disappeared persons' in our midst? We have to act now with the answer, 'not any more!' Such resolution goes beyond the rights or wrongs of diversity and enters the global field of human rights. I cannot do better than repeat what Roshi Naidoo has well said in her essay:

> Though we should take very seriously all critiques of diversity policies, we need to be aware of the political impetus behind some arguments for change. One particular remark in *Boxed In* jumped out at me. Dyer notes: 'There is an equal lazy equation of "blackness" with "disability"…as if blackness were a disability in itself.' Though I understand the broader point about institutions lumping all 'others' together, it is also the case that a political understanding of disability and 'race' have much in common. Disability politics have helped us to understand the ways in which people are made unable to participate in the public sphere, and made invisible in heritage culture, in ways not related to their impairment. The troubling moment in this quote is not just its lack of solidarity, but also the refusal to understand and challenge structural inequalities, in favour of a singular focus on the rights of individual artists.

We have had New Labour and now have the New Conservatives, and, as Naidoo rightly observes, for them 'race politics is simply another interference in our lives, like too many road signs'.

What good is art for this purpose of advancing human rights? Ann Lauterbach, poet, art writer and curator, has expressed very well the cultural effect of art.

> If we understand arts practice as a means to formations of new constituencies of inclusion and belonging that, in [Ralph Waldo] Emerson's great phrase, 'unsettle' our assumptions and realign our relation to the intersecting arcs of our presences, then we will be less vulnerable to the received habits of thought that continue to threaten and curtail our liberties.[7]

10 CULTURAL DIVERSITY, GLOBALISM AND DIGITAL DISSEMINATION

Information is not culture but only a possible conveyance of it. Information and culture have become virtually undifferentiated in the cyberreality transmission that now encircles the world. There is a notion currently cherished that the digital medium of information ineluctably alters the content of culture. Two specific effects of the Web world underpin this claim: intermedial high-density information resources and their deterritorialised dissemination. How do we understand this?

There is no doubt whatever that the advent of the Web has had incalculable impact on all previous media, whether mechanical, electronic or paper-based printed texts. Whosoever is digitally abled can now manipulate all the outputs of information *intermedially*, meaning that every genre of image (moving or still), music, text, 3-D design, database, geological survey, graphic detail, architectural plan, virtual walk-through, and so on, can be manoeuvred into a single digital environment. There is no longer anything like a culturally specific 'original' in these fabulously expanded modes of networked remixings. *Deterritorialisation of data* has released vast hoards of information freely accessible online and this has put intellectual property rights seriously in question. We can speak of interchangeable or 'fungible authorship' but no categorically individual author.

What does all this digitised intermedial fluidity mean? Some art theorists suggest that the ease of expression via global networks has profoundly altered

> differences of power and influence between center and periphery, urban and rural, and traditionally privileged and newly empowered classes. Small-scale and locally based artisanal practices gain enhanced potential. The virtual world, as an ever-expanding experiential, cognitive, sociocultural and economic domain, moves alongside or into competition with the physical environment.[8]

The experience of web-based 'mixed reality' is spontaneously generating on-line cultural communities that will replace the isolated traditionally boundaried ones of the past.

Perhaps so, but the apostles of digital utopia are apt to lose sight of the more sinister aspects of networks. Computer engineering got its impetus from developments in war-time military intelligence, code-breaking, cybernetic control systems, and, not to be forgotten, disinformation, all of which still holds true on a sophisticated scale that far outstrips these origins. Nor should we forget that networking is the essential neural system of global capitalism to which, in the words of the philosopher and social activist Antonio Negri, 'there is no outside' at present.[9] Another cause for concern is that with every welcomed increase of information comes extended paranoiac surveillance.

Artists have the option of digital tools, and those who use them best consciously seem to be the activists alerted to the downside of the global digital regime. The question we must bear particularly in mind in our Report is what potential advances in artistic vocabulary these tools herald for culturally diverse contemporary art practice. Nothing appears to us more contemporary than the instantly mobilised contemporaneity of digital usage. We cannot be satisfied with such a ready-made normalised view of the digital regime which risks taking for granted that its structure is neutrally value-free and not inherently ideological. Artists who take up digital tools in their practice must be imaginatively prepared to assess them and proceed with critical caution to resist the seductions of a phoney electronically commodified universalism by maintaining the specificities of history and the diversities of culture – the most fragile forms of human ecology – that are being eroded to a flat-world level of transmissible information.

We recommend that an advisory council be installed in which artists most adept in 'tactical media'[10] can participate in partnership with administrators, curators and technicians of the art institutions to create programmes that address precisely those 'specificities of history and diversities of culture'. This is anticipated as primarily an art-led research project and not of the conservationist, archival or public educational kind already programmed in many museums and institutional art galleries. We are envisaging once again the future case for creativity in the vast digital territory where there is as yet unimagined scope for institutions awake to the possibilities of forming partnerships with artists engaged in exploring the civil rights issues of surveillance, ecological aesthetics and the avant-garde bio-technology media.

The results of this creative encounter could add a new, entirely unforeseen dimension to what in future we will come to know and share as 'heritage'.

We can foresee the reluctance of activist digital artists to accept the institutional embrace which seems likely to endanger their autonomy. Suspicion of co-option can be overcome by dialogue and by consideration of some models in the past, such as the Art Workers' Coalition in the 1960s, when 'outsider' artists and 'insider' institutional workers realised that they shared similar ideals and goals.[11] Another obstacle, we need hardly say, is funding. But that too is not insuperable if the spirit of partnership is willing to make the necessary effort.

Our view at *Third Text* is that art enjoys a limited, socially indebted but real autonomy that can strive beyond itself to attain new conceptual practices in reality. Are we demanding more of art that it can realistically deliver? Peter Osborne, philosopher and art theorist, has cast the autonomy of art in this light:

> With the decline of independent Left political-intellectual cultures, the art-world remains, for all its intellectual foibles, the main place beyond the institutions of higher education where intellectual and political aspects of social and cultural practices can be debated, and where these debates can be transformed.[12]

That is a good enough place, for now, not to conclude but to begin engaging actively with the creative case in the public sector.

Notes

Introducing the Creative Case

Richard Appignanesi
Introduction: 'Whose Culture?' Exposing the Myth of Cultural Diversity

1   Jean-Paul Sartre, *Search for a Method*, Hazel E Barnes, trans, Vintage Books, Random House, New York, 1988, p 88
2   Ibid, p 90
3   My argument is more fully developed in Richard Appignanesi, 'The future of art in postcultural democracy', *Futures*, vol 39, no 10, December 2007, pp 1234–1240
4   Lucy Lippard, 'Interview with Ursula Meyer' and 'Postface', in *Art in Theory 1900–1990*, Charles Harrison and Paul Wood, eds, Blackwell, Oxford, 1992, pp 893–896, p 895
5   Gerald Raunig, *European Cultural Policies, 2015*, M Lind and R Minichbauer, eds, Iapsis, Stockholm, 2005, p 17, quoted in Richard Appignanesi, op cit, p 1235
6   Gerald Raunig, 'Instituent Practices: Fleeing, Instituting, Transforming', in Art and *Contemporary Critical Practice: Reinventing Institutional Critique,* Gerald Raunig and Gene Ray, eds, MayflyBooks, London, 2009, p 3
7   Stuart Comer, 'Art Must Hang: An Interview with Andrea Fisher', in Mike Sperlinger, ed, *Afterthought: New Writing on Conceptual Art,* Rachmaninoff's, London, 2005, p 32 et passim
8   Ibid, p 41
9   Andrea Fraser, 'From the Critique of Institutions to an Institution of Critique', *Artforum,* vol 44, no 1, pp 278–283, p 282, quoted by Raunig, 'Instituent Practices', op cit, p 6
10 Rasheed Araeen, 'What is Art Education?', commissioned by Greater London Council, 1985, p 11 Sartre, op cit, p 151
12 Ibid
13 Ibid, p 113

Rasheed Araeen
Cultural Diversity, Creativity and Modernism

1   Rasheed Araeen, 'Preliminary Notes for the Understanding of Historical Significance of Geometry in Islamic Thought, and its Suppressed Role in the Genealogy of World History', *Third Text Asia 2*, spring 2009, Black Umbrella/Fomma, London and Karachi, pp 3–14
2   Olu Oguibe, *Uzo Egonu: An African Artist in the West*, Kala Press, London, 1995
3   Rasheed Araeen, 'Conversation with Aubrey Williams', *Third Text 2*, Kala Press, London, 1988
4   Petrine Archer-Straw, *Negrophilia: Avant-Garde Paris and Black Culture in the 1920s*, Thames and Hudson, London, 2000
5   Hans Ulrich Obrist, 'An Interview with Ernest Mancoba', *Third Text 104*, vol 24,

no 3, May 2010, p 373

6   Ibid, p 376

7   Ibid, p 376

8   See 'Beyond Negritude: Senghor's Vision for Africa', special issue, *Third Text* 103, vol 24, no 2, March 2010

9   Obrist, op cit, p 378

10 CoBrA is an abbreviation of Copenhagen, Brussels and Amsterdam. Rasheed Araeen, 'Modernity, Modernism and Africa's Authentic Voice', *Third Text* 103, op cit

11 Laura M Smalligan, 'The Erasure of Ernest Mancoba: Africa and Europe at the Crossroads', *Third Text* 103, op cit

12 Obrist, op cit, p 380

13 Ibid, p 383

14 Ibid, p 383

15 Ibid, p 384

16 Stella Santacatterina, 'Denis Bowen: The Universality of Abstraction', in 'A Very Special British Issue', *Third Text* 91, vol 22, no 2, March 2008, pp 157–162

17 Guy Brett, *Exploding Galaxies: The Art of David Medalla*, Kala Press, London, 1995, p 50

18 Rasheed Araeen, *The Other Story: Afro-Asian Artists in Post-War Britain*, Hayward Gallery, South Bank Centre, London, 1989

19 Rasheed Araeen, 'Art of Benevolent Racism', *Third Text* 51, summer 2000. See also Rasheed Araeen, 'A Very Special British Issue: Modernity, Art History and the Crisis of Art Today', in op cit, pp 125–144

20 Chris Smith, 'Whose Heritage?' The Museums Association Conference, 1–3 November 1999

21 Ibid

22 Ibid

23 Araeen, *The Other Story*, op cit

24 Ibid

25 Araeen, *The Other Story*, op cit

26 Ibid

27 Margaret Thatcher, quoted in the editorial of *Black Phoenix* 2, London, 1978, p 3

The Missing History in Cultural Diversity

Rasheed Araeen
Ethnic Minorities, Multiculturalism and
Celebration of the Postcolonial Other

1   In 2005 Arts Council England launched *Respond: A Practical Resource for Developing a Race Equality Plan.*

2   Rosetta Brooks, 'An Art of Refusal', in Clive Phillpot and Andrea Tarsia, eds, *Live In Your Head: Concept And Experiment In Britain,* 1965–75, Whitechapel Art Gallery, London, 2000

3   See Guy Brett, *Exploding Galaxies: The Art of David Medalla*, Kala Press, London, 1995.

4   Naseem Khan, *The Arts Britain Ignores: The Arts of Ethnic Minorities in Britain*, Calouste
     Gulbenkian Foundation and Community Relations Commission, London, 1976
5   Arts Council of Great Britain, press release, in Rasheed Araeen, *Making Myself Visible*,
     Kala Press, London, 1984, p 161
6   Rasheed Araeen, 'The Art Britain Really Ignores', in *Making Myself Visible*, op cit,
     pp 100–105
7   Rasheed Araeen, 'Preliminary Notes for a Black Manifesto', in *Making Myself Visible*,
     op cit, pp 7–97
8   Rasheed Araeen, 'Art for Uhuru: Some Reflections on the Recent Emergence of Black
     Consciousness in Art', in *Making Myself Visible*, op cit, pp 149–151
9   Osman Jamal, 'E B Havell: The Art and Politics of Indianness', *Third Text* 39,
     summer 1997
10 Ibid
11 Anish Kapoor, letter to the author, 1983
12 There are various references to 'The Other Story' exhibition on the internet. For instance,
     see Philip Lawrence-Hoyte, 'The Other Story (1989)', at http://www.q-artlondon.com
     articles/2-articles/37-the-other-story-1989; and Jean Fisher, 'The Other Story and the Past
     Imperfect', at http://www.tate.org.uk/research/tateresearch/tatepapers/09autumn/fishershtm

Jean Fisher
Cultural Diversity and Institutional Policy

1   Article 27 of the Universal Declaration of Human Rights and Articles 13 and 15 of the
     International Covenant on Economic, Social and Cultural Rights; see http://www.un.org
     overview/rights.html and http://www.un.org/millennium/law/lv-3.htm
2   Koïchiro Matsuura, Director-General, UNESCO Universal Declaration on Cultural
     Diversity, 2001
3   The following are among the most significant of these initiatives: Naseem Khan, The Arts
     Britain Ignores: The Arts of Ethnic Minorities in Britain, 1976, funded by the Arts Council,
     the Calouste Gulbenkian Foundation and the Community Relations Commission (later the
     Commission for Racial Equality), which appeared at the time of an overt breakdown in
     'race relations'; the Swann Report, Education for All: The Report of the Committee of
     Inquiry into the Education of Children from Ethnic Minority Groups, HMSO, 1985,
     prompted by concern at the underachievement of African Caribbean children, and *The
     Arts and Ethnic Minorities: Action Plan*, 1986, both following the violent civil uprisings of
     the early 1980s; the Cultural Diversity Unit of the Arts Council, established in the early
     1990s; *Framework for Change: Moves Towards a New Cultural Diversity Action Plan*
     (consultation document), Arts Council England, London, 2001, which followed the
     Macpherson Report, *The Stephen Inquiry: by Sir William Macpherson of Cluny*, The
     Stationary Office, 1999, on institutional racism and the new anti-racist legislation of the
     Race Relations (Amendments) Act, 2000; *decibel: raising the voice of culturally diverse
     arts in Britain*, 2003, Arts Council England, and the Inspire Fellowship Programme, Arts
     Council England, both concerned with the under-representation of 'ethnic minorities' in
     arts administration; and most recently, *Delivering Shared Heritage: The Mayor's
     Commission on African and Asian Heritage*, Greater London Authority, London, 2005,
     supported by ALM London (Archives, Libraries, Museums), the Victoria and Albert
     Museum and Heritage Lottery Fund, prepared following alarm at the rise in Islamic

fundamentalism after 9/11 and the invasion of Iraq, 2003.

4   Richard Hylton, *The Nature of the Beast: Cultural Diversity and the Visual Arts Sector: A Study of Policies, Initiatives and Attitudes 1976–2006*, ICIA (Institute of Contemporary Interdisciplinary Arts), Bath, 2007

5   Ibid, p 23

6   That in order to acquire agency the generation of Black and Asian artists who emerged during the early 1980s survived initially by *pluralising* their roles – curating, archiving, initiating magazines, critical writing, etc – testifies to the lack of opportunities available to them.

7   'Afro Modern' at Tate Liverpool, 2010, continues this pattern of 'black-themed' exhibitions, when we badly need modernist exhibitions in which historical 'minority' artists are presented with equality and respect alongside white artists.

8   Among the formative policies of the ACE-funded Institute of New International Visual Arts (INIVA) in 1992 was that it should not have a dedicated gallery as this would allow established art institutions to continue their self-replicating policies and hegemony. INIVA's aim was to build alliances with them to produce co-curated exhibitions, an aspiration which mostly failed to materialise. Hylton sees the new INIVA building and gallery as a capitulation to segregation.

9   See note 1, *Delivering Shared Heritage*, Mayor's Commission on African and Asian Heritage, Greater London Authority, London, 2005

10 While the museums' Black History Month may employ more black artist participants and attract more black audiences for one month of the year, there is silence on the level of engagement of white audiences. As *Delivering Shared Heritage* itself points out, there needs to be structural reform coordinated across the entire arts, education and heritage sectors to embed diversity in national consciousness.

11 Jonathan Vickery, *The Emergence of Culture-led Regeneration: A Policy Concept and Its Discontents*, Research Paper No 9, Centre for Cultural Policy Studies, University of Warwick, 2007, p 58

12 Ibid, p 70, my italics

13 Hylton, op cit, pp 127–130

14 Vickery, op cit, p 79

Towards an Inclusive British Community

Roshi Naidoo
Diversity after Diversity

1   Amartya Sen, *Identity and Violence: The Illusion of Destiny*, Penguin, London, 2007, pp 60–61

2   Roshi Naidoo, 'Fear of difference/fear of sameness: the road to conviviality', first published in *Soundings 33*, and reprinted in Sally Davidson and Jonathan Rutherford, eds, *Race, Identity and Belonging: A Soundings Collection*, Lawrence and Wishart, London, 2008, pp 72–81

3   See *Heritage, Legacy and Leadership: Ideas and Interventions,* Cultural Leadership Programme and the Mayor's Commission on African and Asian Heritage, London, 2008,

p 28.

4   Roshi Naidoo, 'Back to the Future: Culture and Political Change', in *Soundings 43*,
     winter 2009, pp 65–76

5   Sonya Dyer, 'Boxed In: How Cultural Diversity Policies Constrict Black Artists', report
     by the Manifesto Club Artistic Autonomy Hub with A-N, The Artist's Information
     Company, May 2007; see http://www.manifestoclub.com/files/BOXEDIN.pdf

6   Ibid, pp 12–13

7   See Jocelyn Dodd et al, *Buried in the Footnotes: The Representation of Disabled People
     in Museum and Gallery Collections*, Research Centre for Museums and Galleries,
     Leicester, 2004.

8   Roshi Naidoo, 'No More Waiting – We Are The Leaders: Assessing the *Heritage, Legacy
     and Leadership Seminars'*, in *Embedding Shared Heritage: The Heritage Diversity Task
     Force Report*, Mayor's Commission on African and Asian Heritage, London, 2009, p 66

9   Ibid, p 66–67

Andrew Dewdney, David Dibosa and Victoria Walsh
Cultural Inequality, Multicultural Nationalism and Global Diversity
Tate Encounters: Britishness and Visual Culture

1   'Black British Art: The Revolt of the Artist', Tate Britain panel discussion, 17 May 2006;
     http://www.tate.org.uk/onlineevents/webcasts/stuart_hall/default.jsp

2   Press release for 'Progress Reports: Art in an Era of Diversity', exhibition held at INIVA,
     London, 28 January – 13 March 2010

3   For the full programme of this conference see
     http://www.vam.ac.uk/files/file_upload/66393_file.pdf

4   For further information about Tate Encounters see the Tate website at
     http://www.tate.org.uk, and the project's archive website at
     http://www.tate.org.uk/research/tateresearch/majorprojects/tate-encounters/,
     and http://process.tateencounters.org/

5   See section 6.34 of 'The Stephen Lawrence Inquiry: Report of an Inquiry by Sir William
     Macpherson of Cluny', The Stationery Office, London, 1999;
     http://www.archive.official-documents.co.uk/document/cm42/4262/4262.htm

6   See section 2.12, Bhikhu Parekh, *The Future of Multi-Ethnic Britain: The Parekh Report*,
     Profile Books, London, 2001; see also
     http://www.runnymedetrust.org/projects-and-publications/publications/29/32.html

7   Ibid, section 3.21

8   See http://www.nationalmuseums.org.uk/resources/nmdc-reports-and-publications/diver
     sity/

9   Munira Mirza, ed, *Culture Vultures: Is UK Arts Policy Damaging the Arts?*, Policy
     Exchange, London, 2006

10   Richard Hylton, *The Nature of the Beast: Cultural Diversity and the Visual Arts Sector:
     A Study of Policies, Initiatives and Attitudes 1976–2006*, ICIA (Institute of Contemporary
     Interdisciplinary Arts), Bath, 2007, p 131

11   The differences generated between the two museums revolve around the distinction
     between National and International Art. To be cast as a British Artist as well as a Black or
     minority ethnic subject is therefore to fall within the British politics of multiculturalism

and its diversity strategies. It is further the case that artists who collaborated with Tate on educational programmes related to the historical collection were often recruited in order to put the other side of the colonial view contained in the collection.

12   This is a complex point that needs more space to expand upon than is permitted here. Suffice it to say that the cultural space referred to is that of digital culture and the expanded visual field, which has established a new default of distributed networks of meaning, which levels subjectivity. In this the cultural worker is a knowledge holder, whose practices of knowledge are contained by the analogical technologies of the museum.

13   Over the course of the Tate Encounters research, the fieldwork period, which involved student participants with a migrational family background in workshops and media productions, was largely understood as a diversity project of Tate Learning, which was a strongly marked department, tasked by the institution with delivering cultural diversity.

14   The results of all of these deliberations are available as audio files on the Tate Encounters archival website: http://www.tateencounters.org/

15   See http://process.tateencounters.org/?cat=6. This discussion was co-chaired by Mike Phillips and Andrew Dewdney.

16   This is a further highly condensed point requiring elaboration beyond the scope of this paper. It is part of the argument about the new conditions of digital culture, in which culture is globally distributed and in which the older hierarchies of knowledge and experience are challenged.

Leon Wainwright
Art (School) Education and Art History

1   As in the popular anthology edited by Kymberly Pinder, where race and ethnicity would be used interchangeably ('"race" here will also refer to "ethnicity" in most instances', she writes). Kymberly N Pinder, ed, *Race-ing Art History: Critical Readings in Race and Art History*, Routledge, London, 2002, p 1

2   As James Elkins has described this development: 'Senses of nationalism or ethnicity have been the sometimes explicit impetus behind art historical research from its origins in Vasari and Winckelmann. The current interest in transnationality, multiculturalism and postcolonial theory has not altered that basic impetus but only obscured it by making it appear that art historians are now free to consider themes that embrace various cultures or all cultures in general.' James Elkins, ed, *Is Art History Global?*, Routledge, Oxford and New York, 2007, p 9. That these older preoccupations have characterised the very foundations of art history and the art idea in post-Enlightenment Europe, and so persist as the ground on which we circulate, goes some distance to explain their abiding presence. (On which see Donald Preziosi, 'The Coy Science', in *Rethinking Art History: Meditations on a Coy Science*, Yale University Press, New Haven and London, 1989, Chapter 4 , pp 80–121; and 'The Art of Art History,' in D Preziosi, ed, *The Art of Art History: A Critical Anthology*, Oxford University Press, Oxford, 1998, pp 507–525. What we have yet to explain more fully is the current style of their articulation as contingent upon art history's sister disciplines and adjacent institutions – including art practice – and the wider field, to museums, mediascapes and the art marketplace.

3   A firm example of this was the key strand on 'Connecting or Competing Equalities?' at the Victoria and Albert Museum and University of Leicester conference, 24–26 March 2010, 'From the Margins to the Core? An international conference exploring the

shifting roles and increasing significance of diversity and equality in contemporary museum and heritage policy and practice.' I gave a keynote address on the subject of 'Diversity and Cultural Policy', alongside Professor Andrew Dewdney of the Arts and Humanities Research Council-supported project, 'Tate Encounters: Britishness and Visual Culture', fully documented at: http://process.tateencounters.org/

4   Quality Assurance Agency Subject Benchmarking Statement for Art and Design/History of Art, Architecture and Design; http://www.qaa.ac.uk/academicinfrastructure/benchmark statements/ADHA08.asp. First drafted in 2002, this statement was redrafted in 2008 with my assistance as a member of the review group. The intention is for the Statement to remain in place for at least another ten years. It forms the basis for assessment of excellence in teaching and learning currently taking place in art and design.

5   Paul Gilroy, *After Empire: Melancholia or Convivial Culture?*, Routledge, London, 2004

6   GLAADH was based at Middlesex University, the University of Sussex and The Open University, and ran from 2000 to 2003. Full details of the project, including reports from its ten sub-projects, and newsletters charting their progress, can be found at http://www.glaadh.ac.uk.

7   See, in particular, section 3.3 of 'Report on the Outcomes of RAE 2001: History of Art, Architecture and Design', Research Assessment Exercise 2001, http://www.rae.ac.uk/2001 overview/docs/UoA60.pdf

8   Olu Oguibe, *The Culture Game*, University of Minnesota Press, London and Minneapolis, 2004, pp xiv–xv. See also Anthony Downey, 'Critical Imperatives: Notes on Contemporary Art Criticism and African Cultural Production', *Wasafiri*, vol 21, no 1, March 2006, pp 39–48.

9   Sean Cubitt, 'In the Beginning: *Third Text* and the Politics of Art', in Rasheed Araeen, Sean Cubitt and Ziauddin Sardar, eds, *The Third Text Reader on Art, Culture and Theory*, Continuum, London, 2002, p 1

10 Paul Gilroy, foreword to Heike Raphael-Hernandez, ed, *Blackening Europe: The African American Presence*, Routledge, London, 2004, p xix

11 To quote Sonya Dyer in full: 'Today, the institutionalisation of diversity policies means that art is being sidelined, and in many cases black artists are first and foremost regarded as black. This is clearly shown by the unhealthy pressure on artists and curators from non-white backgrounds to privilege their racial background above all else in relation to their practice. Black artists and curators are often expected to produce projects that are geared towards attracting a black and minority ethnic audience. One young British Asian curator I spoke to about this said that he had never felt "othered" until he began working in public galleries. It goes without saying that white artists and curators do not generally feel the same kind of pressure to appeal specifically to white audiences.' Sonya Dyer, 'Boxed In: How Cultural Diversity Policies Constrict Black Artists', report by the Manifesto Club Artistic Autonomy Hub with a-n, the artists' information company, May 2007; see www.manifestoclub.com/aa-diversity, p 11. See also: Sonya Dyer, Fiona McAuslan and Tamara Gausi, 'Why are the Arts so White?', *Time Out*, 17–23 October 2007, pp 19–30.

12 Rasheed Araeen, 'A New Beginning: Beyond Postcolonial Cultural Theory and Identity Politics', *Third Text* 50, spring 2000, p 11

13 Michael Hardt and Antonio Negri, *Empire*, Harvard University Press, Cambridge, Massachusetts, 2000, p 194

14 Paul Wood, 'Between God and the Saucepan: A Study of English Art Education from the 18th Century to the Present Day', in Chris Stephens, ed, *The History of British Art: 1870 –*

Now, Tate Publications, London, 2008; D Rushton and P Wood, *The Politics of Art Education, A School Book*, The Studio Trust, London, 1979

15 Grayson Perry, 'Positive Discrimination Patronises Black Artists', *The Times*, 30 May 2007, p 16

16 Martha Rosler, 'Money, Power, Contemporary Art', *Art Bulletin*, vol 79, no 1, 1997, pp 20–24, quoted in Julian Stallabrass, *Art Incorporated: The Story of Contemporary Art*, Oxford University Press, Oxford, 2004, p 21. The first chapter of Stallabrass' study explores in further depth correlations between neoliberal agendas such as those in the arts and those of the wider political economy.

17 I pressed this point in February 2010 when speaking alongside the writer and broadcaster Bonnie Greer and artist Gayle Chong Kwan at a Late at Tate event that complemented the major mid-career exhibition at Tate Britain of works by Chris Ofili. I have also suggested that the Caribbean context ought to be investigated more deeply for addressing recent works by the artist Peter Doig, who also resides in Trinidad: Leon Wainwright, 'Peter Doig, Place and Art History', *Widening Horizons: From the Camden Town Group to Peter Doig*, Education Open Evening, Tate Britain, 29 February 2008 (unpublished presentation). A fuller account of these artists' Trinidad location is given in my exhibition catalogue essay: Leon Wainwright, 'Apples and Grapes from Foreign', in Andy Jacob, ed, *A Suitable Distance: Rex Dixon, Peter Doig, Kofi Kayiga, Chris Ofili and Roberta Stoddard*, Soft Box Studios, Port of Spain, 2006.

18 As Eleonora Belfiore and Oliver Bennett write: '…the traditional impact study may, after all, not be a suitable tool for the exploration of the ways in which the arts affect people. While this might be bad news for cultural consultancies and arts administrators looking for appealing advocacy arguments, it might have the effect of opening up research into the impact of the arts in unexpected and rewarding directions.' 'Researching the social impact of the arts: literature, fiction and the novel', *International Journal of Cultural Policy*, vol 15, no 1, February 2009, pp 17–33, p 30. This is drawn from their larger study, commissioned by the Arts and Humanities Research Council and Arts Council England, E Belfiore and O Bennett, *The Social Impact of the Arts: An Intellectual History*, Palgrave Macmillan, Basingstoke, 2008.

19 Araeen, Cubitt and Sardar, eds, op cit, p 3

20 Slavoj Zizek, 'Multiculturalism, or, the Cultural Logic of Multinational Capitalism', *New Left Review*, no 225, September/October 1997, pp 28–51

Hassan Mahamdallie
Breaking the Code: New Approaches to Diversity and Equality in the Arts

1 Sir Brian McMaster, *Supporting Excellence in the Arts: From Measurement to Judgement*, Department of Culture, Media and Sport, London, January 2008, p 11

2 Donald Kuspit, *An Interview with Louise Bourgeois*, Vintage Books, London, 1988

3 Richard Florida, *The Rise of the Creative Class: And How it's Transforming Work, Leisure, Community and Everyday Life*, Basic Books, New York, 2002

4 Max Nathan, 'The Wrong Stuff: Creative Class Theory, Diversity and City Performance', in *The Centre for Cities*, discussion paper no 1, September 2005, p 1; www.ippr.org/index php?id=78

5   Ibid

6   Jamie Peck, 'Struggling with the Creative Class', *International Journal of Urban and Regional Research Journal Compilation*, vol 29, 2005, p 741

7   Lakhbir Bhandal, interview with the author, 3 March 2010

8   Barbara Gunnell and Martin Bright, eds, 'A New Deal of the Mind Report', in *Creative Survival in Hard Times*, Arts Council England, March 2010, p 23; http://www.artscouncil org.uk/publication_archive/creative-survival-hard-times/

9   Ibid, p 22

10   Bhandal, op cit

11   Ibid

12   Hasan Bakhshi, Alan Freeman and Graham Hitchen, *Measuring Intrinsic Value: How to Stop Worrying and Love Economics*; http://www.missionmodelsmoney.org.uk/papers measuring-intrinsic-value/

13   Mehrdad Seyf, interview with the author, 20 February 2010

14   http://www.disabilityartsonline.org/

15   Colin Hambrook, interview with the author, 10 March 2010

16   In Nancy Hynes, 'Yinka Shonibare: Re-dressing History', and John Picton, 'Yinka Shonibare: Undressing Ethnicity', *African Arts*, vol 34, no 3, autumn 2001, pp 60–73, pp 93–95

17   Terry Rowden, interviewed by Sins Invalid, 12 February 2010, http://sinsinvalid.org/blog sins-invalid%E2%80%99s-interview-with-terry-rowden-2

18   From Dorothy Miles, *Bright Memory*, quoted at http://www.dorothymilescc.org/level2 asp?ID=599&Ref=about

19   Historical note: The black theatre sector in London, desiring creative autonomy and permanence, had lobbied for its own flagship theatre for decades, with collective hopes raised and dashed many times over. The sense of frustration was expressed by actor Hugh Quarshie who was quoted as saying, 'Are we having the agenda set for us by established British Theatre tradition? We measure ourselves by what has gone before. But do I care whether the three sisters get to Moscow?' In July 2005 the Arts Council withdrew support for Talawa Theatre Company's nine million pound project to revamp the Westminster Theatre in central London. A protest meeting was organised and held at the Africa Centre, Covent Garden. In response ACE ring-fenced the remaining capital funds, an inquiry by Baroness Lola Young was commissioned and carried out and a report titled 'Whose Theatre?' followed.

20   http://www.artscouncil.org.uk/publication_archive/whose-theatre-report-on-the-sustained theatre-consultation/. One of those consulted for the report said: 'We do not just need to record our past but revisit it, to show its relevance to our current situation.'

21   Paul Gilroy, 'Britishness, Multiculturalism and Culture – Where Next?', Arts Council Diversity seminar, Tate Modern, Starr Auditorium, 3 May 2006

22   http://www.nationaltheatre.org.uk/51932/platforms/black-british-theatre-archive-at-the-nt html

23   Kwame Kwei-Armah, interview with the author, 20 March 2010

24   *Flesh to a Tiger* (1958) starred Cleo Laine and was directed by Tony Richardson, fresh from directing the Royal Court première of *Look back In Anger*.

25   *You in Your Small Corner*, about a mixed-race, cross-class relationship, transferred to the West End and was then adapted for Granada TV as a Play of the Week. Talawa Theatre founder Yvonne Brewster recalls 'he had this incredible play, *You in Your Small Corner*… Barry was doing what no white playwright was achieving at the time'. http://www.jamaic

gleaner.com/gleaner/20090315/ent/ent1.html

26 At the time David Hemmings was on the brink of Hollywood stardom.

27 Cited in video interview with Barry Reckord, 22 April 1997, Blackgrounds series, Talawa Theatre/Theatre Museum production, Talawa Archive, ref TTC/7/3/5

28 Michael Billington, *The Guardian*, Wednesday 25 January 2006

29 David Edgar, 'On Racism and Modern Theatre', speech, 20 March 2007; http://www.irr.org.uk/pdf/DEdgar_talk.doc

30 Ché Walker, see especially *Been So Long* (a soul/funk musical), Royal Court 1998, Young Vic 2009, and *The Frontline*, (a play based on the life outside Camden tube station), Shakespeare's Globe, 2009

31 Dr Alicia Foster, 'Address to Arts Council 4th Diversity Seminar on Gender Equality', 14 May 2009

32 Linda Nochlin, 'Why Have There Been No Great Women Artists?', *ARTnews*, January 1971, accessed at http://www.mariabuszek.com/kcai/PoMoSeminar/Readings NchlinGreat.pdf

33 Ibid

34 Ibid

35 Ibid

36 Linda Nochlin, interviewed by Martina Pachmanová, 'Art History and Historiography: Writing History "Otherly"', in *Mobile Fidelities: Conversations on Feminism, History and Visuality, n.paradoxa*, online issue 19, May 2006, p 15

37 Janet Wolff, 'Society and the Public Sphere: Strategies of Correction and Interrogation', Pachmanová, 'Mobile Fidelities', op cit, p 92

38 Dr Alicia Foster, op cit

39 Rasheed Araeen, *Art History As A Common Heritage*, proposal submitted to the Arts Council on behalf of Black Umbrella; August 2000; see http://www.thirdtext.com/wp-content/uploads/2009/03/arthistoryasacommonheritage.pdf

Richard Appignanesi
Conclusion: What is to be Done?

1 Thierry de Duve, 'An Ethics: Putting Aesthetic Transmission in its Proper Place in the Art World', in *Art School (Propositions for the 21st Century)*, Steven Henry Madoff, ed, MIT Press, Cambridge, Massachusetts, 2009, p 16

2 Ibid, p 22

3 Florence Derieux, ntroduction to Florence Derieux, ed, *Harald Szeeman: Individual Methodology*, JRP Ringier, Zurich, 2008, p 8

4 Duve, op cit, p 17

5 Louise Jury and Felix Allen, 'Art attack at Tate party over gallery's links to BP', in *The Evening Standard*, Tuesday 29 June 2010, p 5. See also Emine Saner and Homa Khaleeli, 'Crude awakening', *The Guardian*, 1 July 2010, pp 19–22. Platform, a London-based artist-activist organisation, wrote the leaflets which were distributed to the Tate party guests by the Good Crude Britannia alliance. The molasses prank was allegedly carried out by Liberate Tate, an offshoot of the Laboratory of Insurrectionary Imagination. Platform is described as an interdisciplinary organisation that addresses socially engaged arts practice, issues of ecology and social responsibility and delivery of an education programme. Arts Council funding is to support core costs. It has received £16,465 in

2008/2009, £54,145 in 2009/2010, and £59,700 due in 2010/2011. Laboratory is not a regularly funded organisation but has received Grants for the Arts from the Arts Council.

6   Sir Nicholas Serota, 'Don't let a golden age turn into cultural recession', *London Evening Standard*, Thursday 15 July 2010, p 15

7   Ann Lauterbach, 'The Thing Seen: Reimagining Arts Education for Now' in *Art School*, op cit, p 97

8   Jeffrey T Schnapp and Michael Shanks, 'Artreality: Rethinking Craft in a Knowledge Economy' in *Art School*, op cit, p 147

9   Antonio Negri, *The Porcelain Workshop: For a New Grammar of Politics*, Noura Wedell, trans, Semiotext(e), Los Angeles, 2007, p 25

10 *Third Text* has published two special issues of particular relevance to this sphere of contemporary art: *Whither Tactical Media?*, guest editors Gene Ray and Gregory Sholette, Third Text 94, September 2008 and *Media Arts: Practice, Institutions and Histories*, guest editors José-Carlos Mariátegui, Sean Cubitt and Gunalan Nadarajan, No 98, May 2009.

11 Other models are discussed in the *Third Text* special issue, *Art, Praxis and the Community to Come*, guest editor John Roberts, *Third Text* 99, July 2009.

12 Peter Osborne, 'What is to be Done? (Education)', *Radical Philosophy* 141, quoted in Alberto Toscano, 'The Sensuous Religion of the Multitude: Art and Abstraction in Negri', *Third Text* 99, vol 3, no 4, p 369

Contributors

Richard Appignanesi, doctoral graduate in classical art history, is an editor of Third Text and reviews editor of the future studies journal *Futures*. He was a co-founder and editorial director of Writers and Readers Publishing Cooperative and Icon Books. He has served as a curator, lecturer and conference organiser for the British Council. He is the author of the fiction trilogy *Italia Perversa*: *Stalin's Orphans*, *The Mosque* and *Destroying America* (1983–1985), the novel *Yukio Mishima's Report to the Emperor* (2003) and other non-fiction writings.

Rasheed Araeen is an artist, writer and the founder of both *Third Text* (London) and *Third Text Asia* (Karachi). He left Karachi for London in 1964 and has lived there since. In 1965 he pioneered minimalist sculpture in Britain. He began writing in 1975 and then publishing his own art journals: *Black Phoenix* (1978), *Third Text* (1987) and *Third Text Asia* (2008). He has curated two important exhibitions: 'The Essential Black Art' (1987) and 'The Other Story' (Hayward Gallery, 1989). He is now directing a project that will produce the most comprehensive and inclusive history of art in postwar Britain, 'The Whole Story: Art in Postwar Britain'.

Andrew Dewdney is a Professor of Media at London South Bank University and the Principal Investigator of 'Tate Encounters: Britishness and Visual Culture'. He has been Chair of the Arts Council's Photography Panel, Director of Photography and Exhibitions at Watershed Media Centre and is a Director of the Digital Arts Development Agency.

David Dibosa trained as a curator, after receiving his first degree from Girton College, Cambridge. He was awarded his doctorate in Art History from Goldsmiths College, London. During the 1990s he curated public art projects. Since 2004 he has been a Senior Lecturer in Fine Art Theory at the University of the Arts London. His research interests focus on art and cultural difference.

Jean Fisher is a former editor of *Third Text* who has written extensively on contemporary art and post/colonial issues and contributed essays to many anthologies and biennial catalogues. She lectures at the Royal College of Art and is Professor of Fine Art and Transcultural Studies at Middlesex University.

Hassan Mahamdallie is a Senior Strategy Officer at Arts Council England and has a background in theatre. He writes and lectures on issues of race, religion and the history of black people in the West; he contributed to the book *Tell It Like It Is: How Our Schools Fail Black Children* (2005). His biography of radical artist William Morris, *Crossing the River of Fire*, was published in 2008.

Roshi Naidoo is an Arts and Heritage consultant and a Research Affiliate at Keele University. She writes on issues of cultural politics, social justice, heritage and national identity, and is the co-editor of *The Politics of Heritage: The Legacies of 'Race'* (2005). She has worked on projects for varied organisations including the National Portrait Gallery, Museums, Libraries and Archives, the National Maritime Museum, the Greater London Authority and the Institute of Commonwealth Studies.

Tony Panayiotou has been Director of Diversity, Arts Council England since April 2003; he leads the Arts Council's work on race, disability and gender equality and is in the process of developing a Diversity Strategy for the Arts. He started his career in the Race Relations Unit in the London Borough of Hackney and later became the Council's Refugee Officer. In 1991 he joined Hackney's Central Policy Unit. He then spent six years at the National Association of Citizens Advice Bureaux; his last position was Assistant Director of Planning and Performance.

Leon Wainwright is Reader in History of Art at Manchester Metropolitan University. He is a member of the editorial board of *Third Text*, and has held visiting fellowships at the University of California, Berkeley and the Yale Center for British Art. With Charles Harrison and Paul Wood he is co-editor of the forthcoming volume *Art in Theory: The West and the World 1400–2000* (Wiley Blackwell), and author of *Timed Out: Art and the Transnational Caribbean* (Manchester University Press, 2011).

Victoria Walsh is Head of Public Programmes at Tate Britain and Co-investigator of the AHRC funded research project 'Tate Encounters: Britishness and Visual Culture'. In addition to her curatorial work and research projects at Tate, she has worked as a freelancer for the BBC, Mayor's Cultural Office, Architecture Foundation, London School of Economics, and Foster and Partners.

Further Reading

Araeen, Rasheed   'Conversation with David Medalla', *Black Phoenix*, no 3, London,
Spring 1979
——————— *Making Myself Visible*, Kala Press, London, 1984
——————— *The Essential Black Art*, exhibition catalogue, Chisenhale Gallery/Kala
Press, London, 1987
——————— *The Other Story*, exhibition catalogue, South Bank Centre, London, 1989
——————— 'From Primitivism to Ethnic Arts', *Third Text 1*, autumn, 1987
——————— 'Conversation with Aubrey Williams', *Third Text 2*, winter 1987/88
——————— 'Conversation with Avinash Chandra', *Third Text 3/4*, spring/summer 1988
——————— 'Rasheed Araeen and Eddie Chambers 'Black Art: A Discussion', *Third
Text 5*, winter 1988/89
——————— 'Our Bauhaus Others' Mudhouse', Special Issue: Magiciens de la terre,
Editorial Article, *Third Text 6*, spring 1989
——————— 'Conversation with Kumiko Shimizu', Special Issue: 'The Other Story:
AfroAsian Artists in Postwar Britain', *Third Text 8/9*,
autumn/winter 1989
——————— 'The Other Immigrant: The Experiences and Achievements of AfroAsian
Artists in the Metropolis', Special Issue: Art and Immigration, *Third Text
15*, summer 1991
——————— 'The New Beginning: Beyond Postcolonial Cultural Theory and Identity
Politics', *Third Text 50*, Spring 2000
——————— 'The Art of Benevolent Racism', Special Issue: Obscene Powers:
Corruption, Coercion and Violence, *Third Text 51*, summer 2000
——————— 'A Very Special *British* Issue? Modernity, Art History and the Crisis of
Art Today', A Very Special British Issue, *Third Text 91*, vol 22, no 2,
March 2008
——————— 'Modernity, Modernism and Africa's Authentic Voice', Special Issue:
Beyond Negritude – Senghor's Vision for Africa, Guest Editor: Denis
Ekpo, *Third Text 103*, vol 24, no 2, March 2010
——————— Art Beyond Art, Third Text Publications, London, 2010
Bailey, David   with Sonia Boyce, 'The Living Archive Papers: An Introduction', *Third
Text 54*, spring 2001
Brett, Guy   *Exploding Galaxies: The Art of David Medalla*, Kala Press, London,
1995

————————— 'A Tragic Excitement: The work of Aubrey Williams', *Third Text* 48, autumn 1999

————————— 'Tissues of Thought: Performance and Some Other Works in London 1970–1985', *Third Text* 91, vol 22, no 2, March 2008

Checketts, Lynda   'British Art in a Century of Immigration', *Third Text* 15, summer 1991, Special Issue: Art and Immigration

Coutts-Smith, Kenneth   'Some General Observations on the Problems of Cultural Colonialism', *Black Phoenix*, no 2, Summer 1978; reprinted as 'Cultural Colonialism', in *Third Text* 58, vol 16, no 1, March 2002

Drower, Jill   'The Exploding Galaxy', *Third Text* 91, vol 22, no 2, March 2008

Fisher, Jean   *Global Visions: Towards a New Internationalism in the Visual Arts*, ed, Kala Press/INIVA, London 1994

————————— *Vampire in the Text: Narratives of Contemporary Art*, Institute of International Visual Art, London 2003

Gilroy, Paul   'Cruciality and the Frog's Perspective: An Agenda of Difficulties for the Black Arts Movement in Britain', *Third Text* 5, winter 1988/89

————————— 'Art of Darkness: Black Art and the Problems of Belonging to England', *Third Text* 10, spring 1990

Gooding, Mel   'Grace Abounding: Bowling's Progress', *Third Text* 31, summer 1995

Hall, Stuart   'Whose Heritage? Un-settling "The Heritage", Re-imagining the Post-nation', *Third Text* 49, winter 1999/2000

Kapur, Geeta   'Francis Newton Souza: Devil in the Flesh', Special Issue: 'The Other Story: AfroAsian Artists in Postwar Britain', *Third Text* 8/9, autumn/winter 1989

Maharaj, Sarat   'The Congo is Flooding the Acropolis', *Third Text* 15, summer 1991, Special Issue: Art and Immigration

Mercer, Kobena   'Black Art and the Burden of Representation', *Third Text* 10, spring 1990

————————— 'Ethnicity and Internationality: New British Art and Diaspora-Based Blackness', *Third Text* 49, winter 1999/2000

Moody, Cynthia   'Ronald Moody: A Man True to His Vision', Special Issue: 'The Other Story: AfroAsian Artists in Britain', *Third Text* 8/9, autumn/winter 1989

Mullholand, Neil   'Self-conscious Stateless Nation: Neoconceptualism and the Renascence of Scottish Art', *Third Text* 91, vol 22, no 2, March 2008

Nead, Lynda   *Chila Kumari Burman: Beyond Two Cultures*, Kala Press, London 1995

Oguibe, Olu   *Uzo Egonu: An African Artist in the West*, Kala Press, London 1995

Overy, Paul   'After a Long Silence: The work of Li Yuan-chia', *Third Text* 55, summer 2001

Roberts, John   'Interview with Sonia Boyce', *Third Text* 1, autumn 1987

Santacatterina, Stella	'Denis Bowen: The Universality of Abstraction', *Third Text*, 91, vol 22, no 2, March 2008
Shemza, Mary	'Anwar Jamal Shemza: Search for Cultural Identity', Special Issue 'The Other Story: AfroAsian Artists in Postwar Britain', *Third Text* 8/9, autumn/winter 1989
Steyn, Juliet	'The Cultural Politics of Friendship', Special Issue, The Balkans. Guest Editors: Louisa Avgita and Juliet Steyn, *Third Text* 85, vol 21, no 2, March 2007
————————	'Mods, Yids and Foreigners', *Third Text* 15, Special Issue: Art and Immigration, summer 1991
Streicher, Hiltrud	with Uzo Egonu, 'Reflections of Uzo Egonu', Special Issue: 'The Other Story: AfroAsian Artists in Postwar Britain', *Third Text* 8/9, autumn/winter 1989
Hourahane, Shelagh	'Homeland and Foundland: The Sculpture of Avtarjeet Dhanjal', Special Issue 'The Other Story: AfroAsian Artists in Postwar Britain', *Third Text* 8/9, autumn/winter 1989
Tawadros, Gilane	'Beyond the Boundary: The Work of Three Black Women Artists in Britain', Special Issue 'The Other Story: AfroAsian Artists in Postwar Britain', *Third Text* 8/9, autumn/winter 1989
————————	'Black Women in Britain: A Personal and Intellectual Journey', Special Issue: Art and Immigration, *Third Text* 15, summer 1991
————————	'Sutapa Biswas: Remembrance of Things Past and Present', *Third Text* 22, spring 1993
Wainwright, Leon	'Frank Bowling and the Appetite for Pop Art', *Third Text* 91, vol 22, no 2, March 2008
————————	'Back to Black: Art, Cinema and the Racial Imaginary', *Third Text* 78, vol 20, no 1, January 2006

For unpublished documents see Black Umbrella archive at www.thirdtext.com